CONTENTS

v

FOREWORD

In these days of evidence-based medicine it looks as though the death rate from induced abortion in this country has fallen following liberal legislation. The rate would probably have fallen considerably even without such a policy. But perhaps the policy had to happen because some elements of our society were forcefully demanding it while others of us were asleep.

We are ignorant on how much the policy has contributed to the changed statistics and we have hardly attempted to measure the cost in terms of complications. The evidence accepted by our society consists only of what we decide to measure and there are consequences of our behaviour which we can not measure even if we wish to do so. We know some people suffer post abortal depression many years later, long after follow up has ceased and that they are often unwilling to talk about it with their doctor. We don't know all the factors contributing to the disintegration of relationships within society and the family, to the loss of faith in God, to violence and to the abuse of women and children. There is no evidence that abortion has limited these and it may have added to them.

In this country we are clever at damage limitation – or have been so far. When our technology, stripped of these controls, as well as of God-centred ethics, is released on the poor people of the world we can expect to see an increase in the complications of the procedure. These are likely to include the infections that attend a free sex lifestyle, especially AIDS, and these complications are likely to contribute to the very poverty that causes the population problem.

Ann Bell and her husband, a Church of England priest, have seen some of the consequences of legalised abortion at parish level. They have not recorded statistics but they have felt some of the consequences in other people's lives. Ann has also painted many pictures to tell the story. Some of them are reproduced in the book in black and white. When she showed them to me she was moved with real emotion.

It is difficult to speak of a subject like this without being seen to stir up pain but if there is pain to be stirred up it must have a cause. This cause needs to be exposed if it is to be healed and the pain permanently relieved. This healing has been part of her joint ministry with her husband. Her book is more like a painting than a textbook. She knows the people for whom she is writing. May this book be a source of healing and protection for those who read it and for their families.

David R Clegg FRCOG
Overseas Support Secretary of the Christian Medical Fellowship
General Secretary of the Medical Missionary Association
(These views are his own)

INTRODUCTION

It is not easy to commune with God in a strongly materialistic age. When people accept God as their creator, they have to confront disconcerting truths – not least the fact that they have complete free will. The most effective way of eradicating vices and selfish tendencies is to surrender oneself wholeheartedly to God, humanity's supreme Saviour. Yet the prospect of such a surrender can make people nervous. After all, it subjects their bodies, minds and souls to the will of God. In a strongly motivated sexual age, no one feels that challenge more acutely than those women who try to maintain such virtues as chastity and purity with a conscience.

St. Paul throws down the gauntlet in his letter about God's commandments to the Thessalonians:

> What God wants is for you all to be holy. He wants you to keep away from fornication, and each one of you to know how to use the body that belongs to him in a way that is holy and honourable, not giving way to selfish lusts like the pagans who know not God . . . We have been called by God to be holy, not to be immoral. (1 Thessalonians 4:3-8)

It is hard to accept his advice in today's apparently sophisticated world. Often, it seems easier simply to dismiss it as impractical.

The feminist movement is beginning to make the average woman feel oppressed, and yet few are willing to express their anger openly. Those who enjoy their roles as wives or mothers or

1

simply exerting their femininity ought to be attending feminist meetings and conferences, and putting up some resistance to those who adhere wholeheartedly to the feminist creed and who are challenging the Church and faith of Christ. Within the Church, some factions are trying to reinvent belief in the Christian gospel without considering the will of God. In the wider society, many public figures claim to speak for women in the Church and society as a whole. If such people are not challenged by the women they claim to represent, they will succeed in imposing their minority view of the Church and society upon the silent majority.

In a general reassessment of patriarchal Church teaching, women are looking for the right approach to the family and 'reproductive rights'. Many are dismayed to find that abortion can often be accompanied by infection and perforation; that spontaneous miscarriage is placed in the same category as abortion; and that the use of contraceptives can delay child-bearing late into a marriage, resulting in complicated births. Unhappily, such discoveries can result in violent confrontation between opposing ideologies.

Most of those who adhere to a religious faith accept that there is no truth, no freedom and no peace except through Christ and His Church. But the militancy of the feminist and pro-abortion lobbies tends to make quieter wives and mothers retreat rather than put up any opposition. Their hearts sink when the opposing sides in the abortion debate clash violently. They flinch at the feminist call for freedom from oppression for all women and the demand for all women to have full participation in all aspects of life and the Church. Women are encouraged to believe that they have the right to decide on all aspects of their lives, and therefore, to full control over human reproduction. Many of these ideals may have much to commend them, yet they have obscured the reality of Christ's teaching to such an extent that no one is prepared to give serious consideration to the effects of the physical and psycho-spiritual forces which are unleashed by the removal of a child from the womb by medical means in order that the child should be born dead – in other words, abortion.

Many women are happy to go along with what their family

doctors suggest. Yet their unquestioning trust can result in an agreement to have an abortion. Women need to understand the full implications of conceiving, bearing and rearing a possibly unwanted child. They deserve greater support, and a better knowledge of the impact that pregnancy has on the female body and psyche.

This book sets out to present the implications of abortion and artificial contraception, and to put them in the context of Christian faith. It aims to explain the practical issues without being academic or technical. It speaks for those who find it hard to understand the constant debate that surrounds women in relation to contraception and childbirth.

I am not myself a medical expert, but it is obvious that women in general are being kept ignorant of matters that are integral to their physical and spiritual well-being. Increasingly, they are being led to trust 'experts' to make decisions on their behalf. Counsellors, however, always try to help a woman to come to her own conclusion on the basis of full information and without outside influences. This book sets out to provide such information in a language that the ordinary woman can understand and relate to her daily life.

1

Medical ethics in relation to the wombs of women

Present-day outlook

"No," said a young friend as she flicked through a medical book on family planning, conception and childbearing. "It all goes straight over my head. It means nothing to me." She had just got married, but her outlook was not unusual in the circles she moved in.

Where have we gone wrong? How can we overcome such deliberate ignorance in an age that is obsessed with sex? Doctors, midwives, let alone family planning clinics, do their level best to inform the public about these issues. But do they touch on the structure and psychological effect of women's wombs on their metabolism? I wonder.

All women know that there are times when they become emotionally unstable, such as at puberty, during pregnancy and the menopause, and immediately before the onset of each menstrual cycle. Many of us recognise this as a sign that our hormones are playing up, yet we tend to talk in terms of tension and moods, rather than seek a deeper understanding of this hormonal effect on our bodily system.

Media coverage has encouraged us to believe that premenstrual tension can lead to impetuous actions, and even to criminal acts for which women cannot be held responsible. Yet no attempt is made to teach women to protect and respect its source, the womb – a vulnerable part of the female anatomy that is capable of such wonderful things.

Instead, the monthly cycle is seen as a challenge that should be met head-on, with little gentleness or compassion – despite the fact that it holds so many mysteries in relation to our own personalities. How are we to reach out and train men and women to respect and study this strange physical event that can achieve so much that is positive, and yet which can also have such a devastating effect on our emotions and actions?

It is now not uncommon for some women to feel repelled by their wombs. Such women see a hysterectomy, or removal of the womb, as a cleansing operation. A traditionalist, on the other hand, can become almost distraught with fear and anger if such an operation is even mentioned. Many homes are prey to the moods and tensions of menstruating females whose natural reproductive cycle has been set off-balance by increased exposure to sexual hormones found in the oral contraceptive pill or prescribed as treatment for an ever-growing range of medical and gynaecological conditions. Surely it is time for women to look for some answers.

What is a womb?

Most people think of the womb as the uterus. In fact, there is a subtle difference. The word 'womb' means a place in which anything may be formed or produced, while 'uterus' can be defined as an organ that serves as a resting-place for the ovum while it develops into an embryo or foetus. Despite the precision offered by the use of the term 'uterus', 'womb' tends to be much more widely used as it is more loosely defined, and so is much more easily abused.

A more precise explanation of the function of the uterus, or womb, describes it as a hollow, muscular organ lying between the bladder and rectum with connections to the Fallopian tubes and vagina. Most people are familiar with the functions of these organs, for all areas of the media – whether television, radio or written – are unceasingly fascinated by birth and creation. The only way to stem the flow of words is to mention the word 'embryo', which conflicts with the general tendency by women

5

to use the term 'baby' from conception. People are aware that the development of an embryo leads eventually to a human being, but they are unwilling to discuss the daily abuses to which the embryo is subject.

It can be hard for a woman who finds she is pregnant to accept that a foreign body has implanted itself in her body. To many women, the very idea is totally repugnant, particularly if it is unplanned. The sexual revolution has led men and women to accept that the reproductive nature of sexual activity is under control. In fact, the statistics on abortion reveal a quite different situation.

Nevertheless, we need to respect the unique role played by this extraordinary, complex organ, the womb. It is composed almost entirely of muscle, together with a small quantity of fibrous tissue. I wonder how many people are aware that the uterus, like the heart, intestine and blood vessels, cannot be consciously controlled in the same way as limbs or eye-muscles.

The womb is perfectly adapted to its task. The uterine walls are lined with a mucus membrane, or layer of glandular tissue, which in pregnancy is used by the foetus. This layer is shed monthly at menstruation, except when pregnancy occurs, when hormonal changes ensure its conversion into a deeper welcoming layer of tissue necessary for the continuation of the pregnancy. The uterus and the cervix or neck of the womb are attached by ligaments that allow some movement and become more lax during pregnancy and childbirth. All of this careful preparation is supported by a healthy blood supply from the main blood vessels in the pelvic area, which can increase to many times its volume during pregnancy.

Most women are uncomfortably aware of their moods and tensions, but are not likely to connect them with the reproductive organs. The nervous system gains in complexity in this part of the body, and is particularly sensitive to menstruation, pregnancy and childbirth. The sensations are similar to those which emanate from the intestine. In other words, the uterus responds to stretching.

Surely this carefully planned structure should be treasured and nurtured, as an unbreakable link between the acceptance of the

6

existence and order of God in creation and the unique value of human life. It is so easy for people to take it for granted, just as they fail to understand the complex muscle-action it takes to make us smile – though they are horrified if an acquaintance cannot achieve this simple action.

Ovulation and guardianship

Since the unfertilised ovum or egg can only survive approximately 12 hours, with a maximum of 24 hours, fertilisation occurs generally on the fourteenth day of a regular 28-day cycle, while sperm may survive three days or longer. Because the length of the cycle, and therefore the day of ovulation, can vary, a woman should consider herself to be most fertile from seven days mid-cycle. However, this cyclical method of estimating the fertile period is not always accurate if a woman's cycle is irregular.

Sperm from the male can only survive in the female's genital tract between 48 and 72 hours, and it has been calculated that the sperm's journey from the cervix to the outer end of the Fallopian tubes can take less than one hour. Fertilisation is therefore unlikely unless intercourse occurs one or two days before or immediately after ovulation. This highly organised programme of events is set in train by the woman's hormones and her Fallopian tubes. Yet, today, it is considered acceptable to let artificial contraceptives interfere with it. More caution is vital.

I picture the Fallopian tubes as a pair of guardian ducts attached to the upper and outer covers of the uterus. Their function is not only to guard the opening close to the ovaries, but also to help sweep the ovum into the tube leading to the uterus, or tubal canal. The tubes consist of a thick muscular coat that surrounds a highly complex lining of mucus membrane which secretes special material to nourish the sperm and subsequently the fertilised ovum. This delicate mucus membrane can easily be damaged by infection resulting from venereal disease, abortion and childbirth, thus hindering or preventing the passage of the fertilised egg.

The ovaries are located on either side of the pelvic girdle, which protects them, and are found below the fimbriated end of the Fallopian tubes. In size and shape they compare to almonds, and as ovulation recurs over the years, tiny scars form on their surface until they shrivel and wrinkle at the time of the menopause. The ovaries have two main functions: to produce ova and to manufacture oestrogen and progesterone, the two hormones which control fertility.

What are oestrogen and progesterone?

In its natural form, oestrogen promotes the development of female sexual characteristics, besides stimulating egg production and preparing the lining of the uterus for pregnancy. Although many people are aware of the ability of scientists to produce synthetic hormones that mimic the work of oestrogen, many are unaware of the full implications of what has been achieved. Man-made and natural oestrogens and progesterone are used in pills and injections for contraception and various gynaecological conditions.

Responsibility for the long-term effects of such medication needs to be placed firmly with the medical profession. Doctors are only too aware, after their long and arduous training, of the power of oestrogen as it develops in a young girl's body, shaping the breasts, her height and weight, and contributes to the other visible changes in her body contours. As an art student I remember modelling a 16-year-old model in clay. Our entire class was surprised to have to apply more clay as her body developed before our eyes over a period of several weeks.

Progesterone is made by the *corpus luteum* or yellow body that remains in the ovary after ovulation. When the *corpus luteum* dies, menstruation occurs. In pregnancy, the *corpus luteum* lasts longer until progesterone production is taken over by the placenta.

Both of these hormones are ultimately controlled by the pituitary gland which is a master gland situated at the base of the brain. Pituitary hormones stimulate other glands to release their

8

own particular hormones, and there is a 'feed-back' control system to keep the concentration of each hormone in the blood at the right level. Anterior lobe hormones work throughout the body, controlling the activities of other glands, including those responsible for milk flow, and promoting bodily growth. The posterior lobe hormones, on the other hand, regulate the bodily water balance and uterine contractions in childbirth. Finally, the anterior pituitary gland is regulated by the hypothalamus of the brain and this is linked to both the nervous and the hormonal system.

So women, in spite of having bodies uniquely adapted to create, have to accept that the delicate balance required can easily be distorted by the artificially created hormones that are in widespread use in order to allow women to assert their own free will. Whether family planning is achieved by natural or artificial means, it must be seen as exerting a stewardship of God's creation.

In developing nations, some women hardly ever menstruate because they are always pregnant or breast feeding. The resultant high birth-rate is balanced by a high infant and child mortality rate. This outlook can be thrown out by the advent of modern medicine and as economic development reaches them, reducing the mortality rate.

We should at least be aware that our normal brain activity can be influenced by critical fluctuations in the hormonal balance during early pregnancy, and that it is dangerous to interfere and administer additional hormones at this stage. Even so, the dictates of science are getting ascendancey. The chilling stories of ultrasound scans which show unborn babies with swollen external genitalia are the result.

Women tend to avoid most drugs in early pregnancy while the foetal organs are developing, yet they cannot avoid the abortifacient action of the hormone-based contraceptive pill. In addition to suppressing ovulation and rendering the cervical mucus impenetrable to the sperm, it renders the lining of the uterus inhospitable to the developing embryo.

Most women do experience the desire to have a child at some point, and so hormones are also brought into play in order to

9

combat infertility or to reverse a woman's tendency to spontaneous abortion. A wider understanding of the implications of such hormone-based treatments needs to be offered to young women so that they can exert a greater stewardship in relation to childbearing. Where should they turn? Surely, the medical profession should be their first recourse: its representatives are there to heal and guide, perhaps most of all in the field of family planning. Yet even this profession is now at risk, because a legal formula has been imposed on society 'for our own good'.

How can we resolve such problems? Does the contraceptive pill answer all the issues raised by an unplanned pregnancy? Or should the contraceptive pill more properly be seen as a temporary medical deprivation of young girls and women? Surely the doctors should provide answers to these questions. Yet the role of doctors has changed over a period of years. Personal friendship between doctors and patients is no longer the norm. Instead, the doctor's sole involvement is his or her legal obligation to care for the patient's physical well-being.

The womb and the doctor

Let us first turn our attention to Galen of Pergamum (129-199AD), a celebrated physician in Ancient Greece who rose to be court physician in Rome under Marcus Aurelius. He had a deep understanding both of the theory and practice of medicine, and his philosophical outlook was put to good use in the diagnoses and prognoses of conditions. Even today, the following extract from his writings gives a firm and authoritative message to all of us, whether doctors or patients: 'Why is it that doctors, although they admire Hippocrates, do not read his writings, or if by chance they do, do not understand them, or if they have the good fortune to understand them, do not put those ideals into practice and develop the habit of their use?'

Most people have heard of the Hippocratic Oath, which is understood as safeguarding the doctor/patient relationship. Hippocrates (460-357 BC) was a Greek physician who maintained that an understanding of the body is impossible

10

without some understanding of the whole – body, mind and soul. His name was widely used – so much so that the Hippocratic books, which dealt with all aspects of medicine, show widely differing attitudes which cannot be ascribed to one man. He was undoubtedly not responsible for all that was published under his name. But as history has developed, he has come to be seen as the embodiment of the ideal physician.

Hippocrates was a leading educator about the intimate and complex relationship that exists between a doctor and patient – a relationship which is something above and beyond the diagnosis and medical treatment of conditions. It would be interesting to know what he would say about the assembly-line medical centres of the 1990s. Would he approve of the disappearance of the sensitive family physician and accept contemporary doctors, who rely primarily on X-rays, electro-cardiography and laboratory procedures? Or would he accuse them of over-specialisation and mourn the declining role of the general practitioner?

I believe that both Hippocrates and Galen would be dismayed at today's insensitivity to the lessons of tradition. Without that background, humanity today goes through life in constant fear of death. It is perfectly possible to find people who believe that it is a doctor's duty to keep death at bay for as long as possible, so putting the doctor in an impossible position.

The Hippocratic physician had a philosophy which gave him an understanding of medicine which was linked to his knowledge of health and disease. He would have been given training in metaphysics and theology, in a very different form to that offered today, because he would be expected to accept that humankind has a divine goal. During his training, he would learn to understand the human being as a whole, whether eating, working, resting, at exercise or sleeping.

Today, however, a general practitioner who is consulted about a septic finger will be attentive to the needs of the finger, but possibly not the rest of the patient's body. It would be surprising if his/her attitude were different. I am sure that if Hippocrates was alive today, he would seek out the supporters of the technical approach to medicine and try to persuade them that

11

such an attitude could only survive if it was combined with a sound moral outlook.

It is not generally known that the Hippocratic Oath has not been used since the 1930s. In its place a certain secrecy has arisen, which some interpret as similar to the Masonic movement. In actual fact, the medical profession is governed by the Helsinki Declaration. Although society has failed to realise where the problem lies in the relationship between doctor and patient, it is aware of a deep unease in the medical profession.

Margaret Mead (1901-1978), a US anthropologist, was one of the few people to confront the medical profession and was prepared to declare openly that the Hippocratic Oath provided a turning point in the history of humankind. She went on to say that the oath made a complete separation between the acts of 'killing' and 'curing'. Any doctor who had taken the oath was therefore barred from attempts to make him kill a defective child or leave sleeping pills beside the bed of a terminally-ill patient. Under the terms of the oath, abortion and euthanasia were outlawed, as members of the medical profession defended transcendent human rights against the encroachment of the state. Contemporary society, however, has no ears to hear Dr Mead or the philosophy of Ancient Greece. Instead, obstetricians are encouraged to adopt attitudes which reflect new approaches in political and global thought concerning population statistics, which encourage the global study of policy in the fields of abortion and euthanasia. Research into the opinions of the retired population on the possible legalisation of euthanasia is encouraged by the Government, and it seems increasingly likely that one day people will have a legal option for the discreet dispatch of troublesome elderly parents or relatives.

How can we avoid this scenario? The best way forward must be to return to an ethical system which forms part of a clear legal framework. Most professions like to have a code of ethics which offers proof to clients of dedication and standards. Equally, the public likes to know that professions have a code to which they conform and to which individual members pledge allegiance. Physicians in particular prefer to see themselves not as servants of the state, but of the patient. Their desire to heal and restore the

12

patient to good health needs to be supported by a defined code of ethics which transcends the vagaries of today's disorientated and disorganised society, where people live for today without thought for the future.

A promise which acts as evidence of a steadfast code of ethics must be the best way to protect the skills of the medical professionals and those they care for. And surely one of the most deserving candidates for protection must be the woman's womb, the seat of creation. Such a promise would oblige doctors to protect a woman's reproductive organs, rather than prescribe drugs which facilitate sexual activity, possibly outside marriage, and which can harm the woman's reproductive ability. A fresh appraisal would have to be carried out to establish what such a promise should achieve, but properly constituted it could resist the short-sighted demands of today's society and preserve the wisdom of previous generations. Those who prescribe contraceptive drugs have a duty to ensure that those who use them are aware of possible complications, such as the direct effect on physical health such as thrombosis, a possible increased exposure to sexually transmitted diseases and the infertility which might ensue, cancer of the cervix and so on. Women should also be warned against the possible effects on their psycho-spiritual health, let alone on any future marriage or attempt to establish a stable family life.

Perhaps we should study further the unseen forces contained in the feminine contemplative spirit that we call motherhood and which occupy the middle ground between our human consciousness and our subconscious. If used the right way, motherhood can be used as an integrating, healing force, but all too often it is abused. Instead, women have been educated to believe in equality of the sexes. There can be positive outrage when women have to face the primitive forces which appear when confronted by conception and pregnancy, let alone childbirth and the rearing of a child.

This spirit of quiet contemplative thought that is found in motherhood is seen very clearly in the life of Mary, the mother of Jesus Christ. In writing about her, the Apostles are clear that these forces exist, and they point out how Mary waited, reflected and listened throughout her pregnancy. When Jesus Christ was born, there can have been no doubt to observers that Mary had been endowed with the fruits of the Spirit, showing love, peace, joy, gentleness, kindness and most of all patience and forbearance as she faced with awe the task of bringing up an extraordinary child.

2

Maintaining a hormonal balance for the next generation within Christ's teaching

What is a hormone? How necessary are hormones?

Hormones are produced by the endocrine glands and their purpose is to control and co-ordinate our bodily functions. The chief glands are the thyroid, parathyroid, pituitary, adrenal, pancreas, ovary and testicles. The uterus itself is not an endocrine gland, although the placenta acts very like one in some of its functions. You could call them 'chemical messengers of the blood', for they adjust the various functions of our organs in line with our needs. They have become highly sophisticated in the course of evolution, as we can see from the skilful documentaries which appear every so often on television. Such programmes demonstrate the delicate balance of the independent and yet interactive functions of the glands and their close links to the nervous system.

It is the pituitary gland, at the base of the brain, which is key to our considerations, and which co-ordinates all hormonal secretions. The thyroid hormone determines the rate at which the overall physical chemistry operates, the adrenal hormone responds to stress and crises, and the sexual hormones govern the reproductive functions. It is clear from this overview that hormones are highly complex substances which deserve the utmost respect.

Hormones communicate with each other and may influence emotions. However, all humans retain their free will, and the cerebral cortex has overall control. It is hard for a person without medical training to imagine the process of hormonal interaction, but once understood, the implications of disturbing it become more clear. The communicators are made up either of amino acids (the building blocks of protein) or of hormones. These regulate the digestive system, blood sugar levels, blood pressure and fluid balance. A further important function of theirs, which we tend to ignore, is to control our emotions and help the blood system to respond to stress.

It is easier to see these communicators at work in animals than in ourselves. Many of us are aware that some animals change their skin colour when trying to hide, and it is this close link between skin pigmentation and stress which deserves attention. The change is triggered by nervous stimulae which respond to stress in three different ways. The first is to change the colour of the animal's skin, the second releases a stress hormone for flight or combat, the third introduces a morphine-like painkiller. A similar process takes place in human beings, though no change in colour takes place.

These amino acids build special brain hormones or neurotransmitters in the hypothalamus at the base of the brain, which help to regulate our biological clocks. These in turn work together with our sense of sight, smell and understanding to encourage the release of pituitary hormones which directly stimulate the production of sex hormones.

The maintenance of this hugely complex system, which controls our sensual, emotional and reproductive lives, is fundamental to the health of the next generation. The widespread use of artificial hormones can upset the delicate balance of our bodies, possibly at the expense of our descendants. Our natural hormones are uniquely organised to create the child in the womb, and yet we have been taught by present-day society that humanity, and humanity alone, can control the work of our reproductive organs. This outlook results from looking solely at the physical aspects of human reproduction.Try as we might to forget that each of us is marked with God's indelible seal, we cannot relinquish our stewardship of these parts of our anatomy. The key to our redemption and salvation lies in our readiness to accept the responsibility to 'trust and obey'. We must trust the

16

brains God has given us to lead us to the right answers when we follow the principles offered in His Word. Those answers may vary when values rather than facts are applied to the debate. To reach the truth, people need to learn to respect others and recognise their own fallibility.

What would Christ tell us about hormones?

The contraceptive revolution of the 1960s has given women an equal sexual freedom to that enjoyed by men. Over the past two or three decades, many groups have struggled to achieve this goal, and the combined contraceptive pill has been hailed as a landmark achievement in the fight for women's rights. Today, although it is used world-wide, its benefits are in question. Unacceptable side effects have shown the Pill unable to live up to its early promise. Young people, frightened of its long-term effects, are abandoning its use, prepared instead to resort to abortion in the case of an unplanned pregnancy.

Humankind is not willing collectively to acknowledge the harsh reality that abortion, and in particular 'social abortion' (abortion procured for social rather than medical reasons), is probably the greatest evil to win legal recognition in our society. Instead, the destruction of a human life (which in this context is generally referred to as an embryo), is viewed as no more than the disposal of unwanted debris. We strip the embryo of its human value to avoid feeling the pain of its removal, and learn to see the transmission of human life as a mere function rather than a creative act within the cycle of natural order.

Obedience, rather than hormonal balance, lies at the heart of the problem. Through its actions, society is trying to deny the possibility that a person is conceived at conception. Even Professor Edwards, who is renowned for his work with in-vitro fertilisation (commonly called IVF), has openly admitted that he has no answer to the question of when life begins. Should we leave the question unanswered, or should we dig deeper for a solution? Infanticide is something we have always seen as a crime. Yet today, infanticide in the womb is available on demand.

17

All humans began their lives in the mind of God, who is eternal. Christians need to accept their responsibility to work with God in His creation. We need to recognise our own limitations, even those many spontaneous abortions that we cannot prevent. We have to obey, and trust God's sovereignty.

Psychiatrists tend to shy away from asking anyone who has attempted suicide if they have had one or more abortions in the past. Yet numerous people in the caring professions are only too aware that young women can react violently to abortion. Two social issues are simply not addressed: sexual activity and fertility. Instead, society encourages everybody to think they can stay young, healthy and beautiful while at the same time urging them to explore each other sexually and give full rein to powerful emotions such as lust, vanity and greed.

Women are now paying a high price for failing to have a working knowledge of their bodily hormones, or of the full impact of the medicines they take in order to avoid childbirth or an unplanned pregnancy. They need to take account of the world population experts and manufacturers who played down the real impact of steroid hormones in their desire to keep the world's population growth under control.

What do women really want? Surely they want to have healthy children and grandchildren as an outward and visible sign of the love of motherhood. Young people are encouraged to take the Pill and often as a result feel free to engage in teenage sex. But the effect of this is to hinder their natural human development.

If Christ was with us today, he would surely point to Revelation 9:2 'When [the angel] unlocked the shaft of the Abyss, smoke rose out of the Abyss like smoke from a huge furnace so that the sun and the sky were darkened by the smoke from the Abyss and out of the smoke dropped locusts on the earth.' The evils of Pandora's box have been unleashed on the world, and the world is feeling the consequences without being able to understand the cause.

We have listened carefully to the scientists and have acted on their suggestions, but where are we now? They have provided a solution to the devastation inflicted by a plague of locusts by spreading poisoned food among them or by spraying concentrated insecticide over the insects and the vegetation on which they feed. Contraceptives are highly researched and one must accept that in certain circumstances, the Pill offers a safer option than repeated pregnancies. Only in recent years has the evidence of ill-effects apparently been suppressed, particularly in relation to the promotion of condom use and the prevention of HIV infection.

Inappropriate use of the Pill among teenagers is promoted for money, not for population control. One only has to study teenage magazines for evidence of this. The voice of science does try to be even-handed, but in fact science is used by politicians and financiers. Scientists are only too aware of their fallibility. Many of them are committed Christians and one has to conclude that their views are not heard often enough. Regrettably, one must accept that politicians, business interests and the media pervert the truth. This realisation makes women nervous of doctors, and unsure whom to trust.

Numerous women now feel that walls are closing in on them and their reproductive abilities. Certainly, confronted by the complex situation that pregnancy and motherhood now represent, many see abortion as an answer to the immediate problem. Yet on the whole women know that abortion can make it harder to conceive on subsequent occasions, and even after conception all but the most strong-willed are subjected to a battery of tests to ensure that they give birth to children who will be able to support the state rather than act as a drain on finances.

Scientists have tried to study life's beginnings from every angle and to uncover the fundamental principles of fertilisation and the earliest stage of embryonic development. To a large extent, women have become the victims of this research. Yet many people still believe that science and medicine have worked together for the benefit of society in developing contraceptive medicines. It is less common to find an awareness of the fact that the research is testing the moral attitudes of our society by probing every aspect of human life from the very beginnings of matter to the emergence of life itself.

It would have been interesting to hear Karl Popper (1902-

19

1994) the Austrian-born British philosopher of science, addressing a contemporary female audience. He maintained that science was one of the greatest spiritual adventures of humanity. But how many women would support him in his belief that good science involves a process of trial and error where ideas are developed and tested? Those who felt he was correct might well exert pressure to stop the experimentation with hormonal treatments. Popper's response would have been to argue that in the final analysis, individuals and doctors have to make up their own minds about their ethical standpoint. Many lay-people, however, are aware that we are afloat on unplumbed depths without a rudder. Christians know that Christ is our only source of hope.

The Christian and respect for life

If we are to practice good stewardship in the world, we have to show as much respect for our own species as we do for the animal kingdom. Surely, if we are concerned about cruelty to animals, we should also oppose abortion and destructive experiments on human embryos.

Many Christians believe that people tend to discern pantheistic divinities in trees, rivers and hills rather than worshipping God through nature. This type of belief-system side-steps many of the demands of Christian discipleship, but still confronts people with the mystery of life and death in creation, and here only Christ, the redeemer of humankind, can give us clear and concise answers.

Recent advances in reproductive biology have certainly created new issues for those of us who wish the developing baby (or embryo) to receive maximum protection from conception. Careful phraseology is required: the foetus in the womb is a human being with potential and *not* a potential human being.

Sometimes, people forget that God, who understands every aspect of creation, knows that the ultimate in human worth lies in the ability to worship and form a relationship with our Creator. Yet passionate supporters of women's rights and materialism find it easier to distance themselves from this outlook by using medical terminology.

Although humans are probably not meant to understand all the mysteries of life, an attempt is made in the Book of Ecclesiastes to explain the worthlessness and vanity of human life. Its words – which our Lord no doubt studied as a child – have relevance for us today: 'As you do not know the path of the mind or how the body is formed in the mother's womb, so you cannot understand the work of God, the Maker of all things.' (Ecclesiastes 11:5) The attempt to control life is possibly one of the greatest challenges humankind has set itself. Christians should not hesitate to support natural methods of family planning as a method of contraceptive control available to all those who express an interest in knowing how their bodies work. Yet NFP requires an investment of time and commitment from both partners, and some understanding and care must be offered to those who cannot achieve this level of self-control.

Nevertheless, God is concerned about the continuation of the human life which He created, and the Scriptures make it quite clear that children are a gift from God. These days, childbearing is regarded almost as a woman's right, with scientific medicines there to make it possible. We may now be nearer than we think to Old Testament times, when infertility was regarded as a reason for despair and humiliation. Life tends to come in a full circle, and that is what is happening today.

The Bible provides further assurance of the reality of human life in the womb. In the Gospels, while Mary was pregnant, she visited her cousin Elizabeth who was also expecting a child. John the Baptist leapt for joy in Elizabeth's womb, and yet she was only six months' pregnant. Then, as now, the unformed child was sensitive to its creator. In today's agnostic era it is hard to discern the Holy Spirit, yet God's creative power is constant from one age to the next.

3

The way forward – a need for knowledge

The present situation

Although collectively, the United Kingdom considers itself Christian, that view is not borne out by the legislation passed in recent years. For better or for worse, organised religion appears to have become irrelevant to most of us. Instead, we try to make the most of the present – and even the merits of that outlook are wearing thin. Wary of dividing issues into 'right' or 'wrong', we bundle any ethical issues together into a no-go area, in which no one recognises anyone's right to declare what ought or ought not to be done.

Yet Christianity remains an issue, and its principles and morality are constantly in question, denigrated and debased by the national media and entertainment industries. Christians are going through a bewildering and anxious time, and many shrink from any challenge to their faith because they simply do not know how to respond. It seems almost impossible to stop this deliberate degradation of what is pure and good, and so many Christians are having to accommodate themselves to a certain decadence in the society around them rather than compelling people to face uncomfortable facts.

Nevertheless, anyone who believes in God's love for us has a duty to examine critically the roots of the problems we see in our daily lives. Rather than allocating blame to governments, churches, local councils, doctors or scientists, we need to look in a mirror and ask ourselves: 'What are you going to do about it?'

22

Most people would agree that the trend in the United Kingdom and elsewhere in the world towards secularist and materialistic values has reached a critical stage. The state now heaps praise on greedy and selfish attitudes rather than encouraging constructive behaviour, leaving its citizens to talk nervously of a 'nanny state' and to try laughing away the changing climate.

Where can we look for moral leadership now that the state has abdicated responsibility? We should surely turn first of all to the Christian denominations, whose long-established institutions have the authority to provide us with a spiritual vision.

An American rabbi once said: 'When I hear talk of a Christian society, I see barbed wire.' His words hold a valid message which needs to be met head-on. Those of us who adhere to a Christian way of life, whether resident in the UK or elsewhere, have given in to the fear which arises when confronted by this type of opposition. We have systematically hedged ourselves in to increase our sense of security – even to the extent of putting up defensive mechanisms to protect ourselves from all possible harm. This desire for self-preservation lies at the root of our unease. All of us – even those who call themselves Christians – have developed an existence and an outlook which begin and end with ourselves, and which have no external point of reference.

In his letter to the Romans, St. Paul showed that we should seek an outlet from our universal sinful condition through divine guidance. His first piece of advice, however, it is to bow to civil authority. 'Everybody is to obey the governing authority, because there is no authority except from God, and whatever authorities exist have been appointed by God; so anybody who disobeys an authority is rebelling against God's obedience, and rebels must receive the condemnation of the law' (Romans 13:1,2). Most of us find his advice hard to accept, particularly when we can see the state apparently allowing some to benefit from the weakness of others.

St. Paul is deeply aware of the tug of war which is underway between worldly pressures and moral ideals, as embodied in God's Word. The opposing pressures can make people feel riddled with sin. The rabbi's image of Christians surrounded by barbed wire is not far from the truth.

The way forward after reflecting on the outcome of sexual ethics

The sexual revolution and its liberal overtones have exacted a high price from both men and women. Many previously clear issues have become blurred – not least the meaning of 'love'. One question dominates: 'Where do I stand?' The state has transformed greed from a vice into a virtue, and society is now paying the price.

Let us start by looking at the Pill and other contraceptive devices which have been used by women all over the world in probably the most wide-scale scientific experiment ever known. A question-mark now hangs over a woman's role. Is her greatest fulfilment to have healthy children and grandchildren? Should her sexual appetites remain active throughout her lifetime? Why are some healthy young women who take the Pill more likely to develop blood clots and suffer strokes or heart attacks? Should contraceptive aids be offered to couples in sexual relationships outside marriage? Why should sex be promoted at all? Is it right that huge multi-million dollar complexes are cashing in by offering contraceptives which will increase sexual activity?

The questions are endless, but one fundamental development is worth noting. It used to be generally accepted that users of the Pill were twice as likely to divorce their partners. That general rule has been overtaken because of the complexities of sexual relationships both inside and outside marriage. The fact that couples are encouraged to engage in sexual activity before they are emotionally mature has become an even greater factor in the consideration of stable relationships.

The frequent tendency to link Pill-users with the development of thrombosis (blood clots) should be tempered by the knowledge that the risks for all women increase as they become older, particularly if they are smokers. Another risk factor is a possible genetic predisposition to blood clots. The risk posed by an increased dose of oestrogen, to which Pill-users are exposed, is now much lower as the dosage has been reduced.

Many people still offer an answer to all these problems by advocating the word No as the best form as birth control. They

24

are opposed by those who think that this outlook is unthinkable in such a liberated age. The fact is, that there is conflict at the very heart of personal relationships and a lack of respect for the human person is being reflected in the breakdown of family life, and the collapse of good neighbourliness.

Far from enhancing the 'rights' of women, the state's endorsement of social abortion has resulted in less respect for women and a failure to take responsibility for a conception. This outlook has contributed to an increasing fear among women and to abuse in all sections of society, where violence has become a part of everyday life. This diminished respect for life has led to savage attitudes towards the human being at every stage of its development in the womb. Even so, most of us prefer to turn a blind eye to articles about the warfare currently being waged against the unborn or about the tiny embryos which are used in scientific experiments. Even less palatable is the fact that the law allows any unborn child which shows signs of disability to be destroyed up to birth.

Numerous conferences and charitable foundations have tried to address these ethical issues, but nobody has so far attempted to carry out an in-depth study of why motherhood – an essential part of our natural order – has lost its standing in society. Any close analysis would reveal the ugly face of feminism.

The mother-of-pearl, produced by the oyster, has a beautiful lustre and is a highly prized gemstone. It is made up of a calcareous substance secreted by molluscs which is deposited in thin layers on the inside of the shell. But instead of being content with the rare beauty of naturally-produced pearls, we encourage the production of artificial pearls. To create these, a tiny bead of shell from a clam, plus a small piece of membrane from another pearl oyster's mantle (to stimulate the secretion of nacre) are inserted in oyster shells and left to mature in cages for three years before being harvested.

Similarly, motherhood is a very precious thing of enormous value and formed naturally within the female frame. But, as with the pearl, we have sought and found artificial means of controlling pregnancy and childbirth.

The word 'love' has become almost interchangeable with

'sexual intercourse'. Yet in the New Testament, love is central to God's being, and of humankind's response to God. The Greek translation of this much-abused term is literally 'dutiful', 'filial affection', or even 'passionate emotion'. In the New Testament, love is a supernatural Christian virtue which is synonymous with 'charity'.

St. Paul describes the nature and characteristics of love in his hymn to the turbulent Christian community of Corinth (1 Corinthians 13). He describes how all love is drawn first to God, and secondly to ourselves and our neighbours as the objects of God's love. This is the kind of love which is found in motherhood. It is based on selflessness, which is self-giving in its fullest sense. The opposite of this emotion is hate. Women who give their consent for their unborn children to be killed through abortion are opening themselves up to the danger of hating themselves.

The path of standing alone

These days, women and childbearing have become the focus of two academic disciplines: science and ethics. Why? Because the woman's womb is at the centre of the mystery which surrounds human conception and reproduction. Although the scientific revolution has brought enormous changes to men and women's understanding of themselves, it has transformed the face of conventional medicine and posed a challenge to ethical judgements and beliefs which were formerly fundamental.

As biology impinges on medical practice more and more, infertile men and women have been encouraged to hope that they can expect to conceive their own children. But alongside this optimism is confusion. Scientific television programmes reveal that what we had thought to be impossible is now possible, and yet we know that these scientific achievements are shaking the very foundations of organised society. Politicians, doctors and lawyers have been slow to respond and instead have sought to appease the fears of the general public rather than addressing the issues raised. This is not helped by a tendency in the national media to wring a knee-jerk response from the population on any critical issue, rather than present a reasoned and many-faceted deliberation of the known facts.

In spite of the affluence of the society in which we live, where economics serve humanity, deprivation is widespread in the form of marriage breakdown, suicide, loneliness, drug addiction, homelessness, abortion and debt. People are aware that somewhere, our society took a wrong turning, but they cannot pinpoint where or when that was. They want to pass something of value to the next generation – but what? In future, will people have to stand alone in order to resist the pressures of a demoralised society?

In Japan, the birth-rate is the lowest of any developed country, and yet it has one of the highest abortion rates in the world. For each married couple, just 1.5 children are being born. That is not nearly enough to stop the population from shrinking. Sociologists predict that one quarter of the Japanese population will be over 65 by 2025. This lack of children means that taxes will have to rise to cover the cost of future pensions. Single young women are unconcerned by the problem. They are for the most part in full-time work, living with their parents rent-free and with few responsibilities. Once married, however, that serene life style comes under threat: only one in eight married women maintains a career.

On the face of it, the Japanese appear to have developed a successful society. Yet the falling population gives the lie to appearances. The country takes great pride in its sexual equality laws of 1986, which have been implemented carefully and with a strong sense of order. Ahead, however, lies the prospect of a poverty-stricken ageing population, with insufficient people of working age to support them.

A similar outlook prevails in the western world, yet many a good mother will take a low-paid job if it fits in with her family life. The British Government pushes for equality at all levels and yet fails to provide comprehensive day-care facilities for children under school age. Is it right for the Government to maintain this stance, or is it simply making a token obeisance to feminist pressures? If the sexes are to be treated as equal, and both men

27

and women are to be encouraged to keep their careers going alongside their family lives, then the state should take some responsibility for the care of the children.

And yet, if the state does take a greater share in the upbringing of the next generation, the prospect opens up of day-care centres which promote the state view of sexual equality, indoctrinating children from an early age against traditional family life. This trend has already been noted in Scandinavia. If it gains currency, we are in danger of seeing the role of the home-based mother disappear.

Christian men and women need to have the courage to stand together and offer an example of family life. Mary, the mother of Jesus Christ, is our example. We know, and she knows, that she was not just chosen for her physical ability to bear the child Jesus. Although she conceived Jesus Christ through divine grace, she was nevertheless to feel, like us, that tug of love which comes with motherhood. Like her, we have the capacity to reconcile ourselves totally and completely to a child's conception. Mary's example shows how she surrendered herself to her child, and therefore to God, in faith. At each and every conception, we too should nurture and protect the God-given love which is peculiar to motherhood.

Mary stands out as a sign of the distinct quality of the Christian Church. She was 'in place' for God's gift of himself, and he expects no less from us. For all Christians, Mary will always symbolise the eternal feminine, showing the world the uniqueness of the womb, and the order of creation. A woman's reaction to her new-born child is evidence enough of the fact that womanhood achieves a sense of fulfilment through childbirth.

But where does this leave those who do not or cannot give birth? We live in an age when women are encouraged to think of children as a desirable possession, and new mothers show others what an enormous impact childbirth has on them. Yet all women hold within them the capacity to love the innocence of childhood with great passion. There are many ways in which this gift manifests itself in unmarried or childless women, not least through the apparently mundane village Brownies, which are often run by single women.

Our changing society is now rejecting this type of relationship, and children are no longer shared in a communal sense. Children have to be protected from a society which seems to have become increasingly violent towards young life. So the fierce loneliness which surrounds creation continues: more and more, children are seen as possessions rather than human beings in their own right, made in the image of a loving God.

Perhaps childless women have a lesson for others. They have not entered this area of conflict, where men and women are learning to deny the spiritual force which lies at the heart of each human conception. The personal standards of the childless adult are needed by society at all levels. They contribute a dispassionate charity and clarity of vision, which can help others to see and comprehend the sword of Damocles which hangs over each and every human conception.

One category of women often ignored in the debate over abortion is those who cannot conceive and who even so have a burning maternal desire literally aflame within them. After the 1914-18 war, thousands of women who would normally have married and had children could not do so because so many men had been killed in the conflict. Others, whose husbands failed to return from the war, never bore children. Most of them did not waste their time grieving; they poured their maternal love into child-care through parish activities such as Sunday schools, education and numerous other community works. Some went on to found schools which now enjoy a considerable reputation. These women were rich in a way that single women lack today: the wider community *respected* their single status. Unfortunately, such an attitude is now rare. Instead, a woman who has not had sexual intercourse tends to be regarded as an oddity, and a childless couple is encouraged to pursue every medical avenue in order to have their own children. Far from encouraging the single and childless to enjoy the wider family offered by the local community, society ostracises these people who do not epitomise the 'norm'.

Although the 'war widows' of the 1914-18 war had not conceived and reared children, they exerted their motherly love and took pride in using it in their daily lives. Children today are

29

poorer in so many areas of life, simply because single women are no longer able to pour out their love on the children they deal with in their daily lives.

In spite of social pressures, women now have the freedom – some would say the right – to control their bodies and lives. Often, women abort their unborn children not because they refuse to look after the child, but simply because they want to avoid the responsibility of rearing a child and the pregnancy itself. Some argue that to force such women to bear their child and offer it for adoption would mean that they could not express their free will. Yet few give any thought to the fact that abortion cuts off the development of motherhood at its most vulnerable point, and strikes at the very soul of women who choose this course of action.

Today's civilisation has clearly taken a wrong turning, and mistakes have been made in assessing the role of the single woman. Perhaps, in the years ahead, we may be able to rectify this sad scenario by looking for an understanding of ethics and moral concepts. Until that point is reached, society as a whole can only turn to Christ's mother, Mary, and ask for her support, love and understanding as they try to comprehend the unique role she took on for humankind.

Another way of coming to terms with the sin which lies at the heart of individuals and of society is to look for answers in the Cross of Christ. Until society ceases to search for fulfilment of its own desires, and instead tries to follow Christ's gospel, it cannot change for the better. Even if humanity does choose to follow Christ, there will always be some who will resist change. Yet today, it seems that people want to avoid making a decision because they prefer to follow a gospel which is centred around the individual rather than society as a whole.

4

The desire to create life and the conflict
of the sexual revolution

The desire to create

The number of test-tube baby clinics around the world must be in the hundreds, bearing witness to many women's desire to give life to another human being. On the other hand, there are hundreds, if not thousands, of other clinics which offer women the opportunity to expel a potential human being from the womb before it is capable of independent life. For many people, abortion is a means of birth control which, although controversial, is essential in view of the growing world population. The fact that people of goodwill feel this must be extremely frightening for all those of child-bearing age. It increases the pressure on them to present the state with a healthy, flawless child which has the potential for a good 'quality of life'.

On the other hand, if a physically or mentally handicapped child is born, its parents often experience reproving looks from neighbours and friends, while the local health authority wrings its hands at the financial role it will have to play in the child's upbringing. The state has made it quite clear that the birth of physically or mentally handicapped children can be an unwanted financial burden, and couples who defy this attitude can suffer public condemnation for their decision to continue the pregnancy. Yet the love shown by many parents of handicapped children is awe-inspiring.

What force makes women, even those who have been through the menopause, want to bear children? Just as in physics we see energy at work in electricity, light, heat and so on, in psychology too there are intense unseen forces at work. Our psychology is affected by similar experiences and emotions: instinct, heredity, environment and culture; sensation, perception, learning and memory; the bases of motivation and emotion; and our thought, intelligence and language.

Physical and psychological reactions to pregnancy are closely related, and although the process itself is predictable, some women experience a profound alteration in their emotional behaviour. We tend to forget that all women become emotionally unstable when their hormone levels are fluctuating. In an age when equality of the sexes is the ideal, few allowances are made for this fact. Certainly, many women, regardless of their education or upbringing, can feel quite unbalanced during their monthly cycle or pregnancy, and cannot understand or control the forces at work within them.

Despite the warnings of specialist literature, there is a public refusal to recognise that pregnancy can have a significant impact on women's emotions. Yet those working in an office alongside a mother-to-be tell an entirely different story. They know that a pregnant woman can burst into tears without the slightest provocation, and yet be her normal self again in a matter of minutes. The mere idea of a child growing inside her body is sufficient to cause radical emotional swings.

What are the feelings of a woman who wants to bear a child, but is not yet pregnant? For an answer, we should look to our Judeo-Christian heritage which has been the basis for much of our legal framework in traditional western societies. It has placed great emphasis on the intrinsic worth and value of every life, and this fundamental principle has underpinned the medical profession. Today, the belief that every human life is worth saving is being eroded, and the change is having a most unhappy influence on those who want to become parents. It has caused a shift in public policy and has had a profound influence on the attitudes of the public services to pregnancy, as well as to legislation and the teachings of the mainstream Christian churches. The general populace has been encouraged to perform mental gymnastics in order to separate the concepts of abortion

32

and murder. The first has become acceptable, while the second remains abhorrent.

The distortion of fact has progressed so far that people now prefer not to register the fact that a human life begins at conception and is a continuous process, whether intra- or extra-uterine, until death. Doctors and nurses who provide maternal care now find it easier not to become too involved with their patients, however much they love their work. As a result, fewer people are prepared to discuss the mental anguish of women who have undergone abortion and who have at a later stage delivered a fully developed child. So many who attend the birth of a child know the miraculous joy which accompanies the event, but even they have to recognise the divisiveness of the abortion laws which exist to the detriment of the medical profession.

Even academic researchers prefer to avoid studying the part that medicine plays in this radical change of outlook: it involves far too many unpredictable emotions for objective analysis. It is hard not to be anxious that the developing legislation on birth control and birth selection will lead to new legislation which will allow us to control and administer death selectively. The new outlook has even been woven subtly into television programmes. One has only to read the television listings to discover the interplay of life and death in all kinds of programmes which depict the doctor-patient relationship and disorientated family life, let alone the problems of birth and infertility.

The medical profession is essential to the planning and decision-making for our well-being. No other group of people has an equivalent knowledge of human nature and behaviour, let alone health and disease. If we want a society which has developed in a rational and balanced manner, the medical profession – currently under so much pressure to change the very roots of medical ethics – must help us to mould that society. It is in the field of abortion that the medical profession is most vulnerable to criticism. Despite an instinctive awareness that what they are doing is wrong, many doctors agree to perform abortions. The fact that the British government has recently handed over the health services to be governed by the market philosophy has furthered this trend. Those doctors and nurses who object to abortion, whether in hospitals or in general practice, are finding it increasingly hard to find employment. To concentrate on the much more debatable sphere of contraception and the Pill weakens the argument.

The Declaration of Human Rights, adopted by the United Nations in 1959, provides some comfort: 'The child, by reason of its physical and mental immaturity, needs special safeguards and care, including appropriate legal protection before as well as after birth.' Yet since the adoption of this declaration, women in Great Britain have won a new personal liberty – the right to have pregnancy terminated at any time up to 28 weeks, or up to term in the case of handicap. The law varies enormously from country to country. Some nations, such as China, where the disposal of infant girls is commonplace, try to conceal the statistics for fear of condemnation. Others are happy to fall in with the idea of World Health Planning for family life. Yet in Moslem countries, each conception continues to be welcomed with joy.

It seem extraordinary that women are still prepared to carry children despite the pressures exerted upon them by the medical authorities who want to perform endless tests to check for foetal abnormalities. Governments in many countries believe that they need to exert a strong paternalistic influence if they are not to fail in their duty to maintain an orderly and balanced approach to the safety of children in and out of the womb. Over the past 40 years, numerous nations have turned their backs on centuries of wise stewardship and instead have tried to build on new scientific achievements and aspirations. They should now recognise that they have failed.

The conflict of the sexual revolution

Good stewardship lies at the heart of our relationship with ourselves and with the created world. Yet people have not been consulted about the inconsistent approach to life in the womb, and to contraception. Those who are prepared to stand up and be counted know only too well that they must confront an unreasoning anger which can strike out randomly and in any form.

Without doubt, contemporary society puts a very low value on human life in the womb. People are encouraged to put their own desires above the need for an ordered society. Instead of being life-givers, enriched by motherhood with love and generosity, women are now prepared to exterminate the life growing within them just because they do not want to undergo childbirth, do not want to become mothers, or feel indifferent to the life growing within them. Yet, paradoxically, if one challenges a girl whose pregnancy is unwanted and asks her to bear the child and offer it for adoption, she is likely to exclaim: 'If anybody is going to bring up my baby, I will.'

Although we live in a society where almost anything goes, most women who enter into a casual sexual relationship observe an unwritten contract with the partner: 'I will respect your rights and life style if you will respect mine – even if I decide to abort our baby.' But even that respect for the individual can come under threat if society starts denying that a human being is made in the image of God. Without a general respect for the right to life as a fundamental part of the social framework, society is likely to reach a crisis.

Unfortunately, there is a tendency to use education as a political tool, and the result is that teenagers are no longer prepared for the future in the assurance that they are high-quality human beings with as much potential as their neighbour. It is not surprising that young people look for their own solutions to immediate problems, grabbing at one sweet moment and a roll in the hay, just as people used to in earlier centuries.

The Government has sponsored sex education so enthusiastically that it is open to the charge of irresponsibility. Films and television programmes reinforce the Government line, so that it filters through to children whatever the parents' views. The problem now is that an active, satisfying life of sexual activity is viewed as a human right. No one sees the need for either males or females to delay entering into physical relationships. In fact, sex has joined the ranks of recreational activities which are encouraged by modern society's erratic life style.

Nevertheless, love ought to underpin the sexual act, whether it is entered into casually or with commitment. The parental love which ought to guide young people in their fledgling relationships can no longer be counted on. What response can we give a 14-year-old pregnant girl who had sex with a 13-year-old because she received no love at home from her divorced mother and her boyfriend? It takes considerable courage for the mother in such a case to recognise that she, or maybe society, has failed her daughter, to look after the grandchild, and send the daughter back to school. Yet such acts of bravery do occur.

Another consequence of casual sex which most prefer to ignore is the fact that reproductive health rapidly deteriorates. It is not unusual to hear parents, and even grandparents, give distressing accounts of how their children or grandchildren are suffering from pelvic inflammation, have become distressed after the breakdown of a relationship or have had to submit their disturbed bodies to early hysterectomies, so denying themselves the prospect of ever having children.

Is there an answer to these problems? St. Peter, known as the greatest miracle-worker of all the apostles, knew what it meant to live for the love of Jesus Christ. Despite this, he rebelled from time to time, and received sharp rebukes. Even his shadow was said to heal the sick. He would understand our present predicament, and no doubt would repeat to today's society his admonition in Acts 2:38,39: 'You must repent, and every one of you must be baptised in the name of Jesus Christ for the forgiveness of your sins. And you will receive the gift of the Holy Spirit. The promise is to you and your children.'

36

5

The responsibility of government

Why have a government?

What is a government for? It may seem an odd question, but it reflects the West's growing lack of confidence in democracy – an inherited system, rooted in Judeo-Christian values, which no longer seems to be working. Our freedom, as inheritors of a contemporary democratic tradition, has not been easily won. In some ways, western society is rather like an aged man suffering from gout, his blood spoiled by an excess of uric acid and inflammation of the joints. In the same way, western society is ailing after its long-drawn-out fight for survival. Faced with a breakdown of order, people need to ask whether this collapse is a chronic condition. Other countries too boast a similarly strident prosperity which many Third World countries envy and try to copy. It is now all too easy to lose sight of previous generations' legacy of law and order.

The Christian churches let all people down when they failed to unite against the legalisation of abortion. They had ample opportunity to gather data on the effects of abortion on the lives of individuals and on society as a whole, yet their only reaction to the gathering storm was to wring their hands and issue a series of reports. *Did they recognise the child in the womb as their neighbour in Christ?* Does their stance reflect internally divisions about the morality of abortion?

As formal institutions, the churches find it difficult to take a stand when the state is already determined on a course of action.

Having failed to take joint political action for the protection of life, they have increasingly withdrawn into their individual units instead of making a bold united stand against the evil of abortion.

The history of the United Kingdom demonstrates clearly that in a parliamentary democracy, priests or ministers are unlikely to be encouraged to challenge public officials. The spirit of autocratic Henry VIII remains with us. He opened the door to the Reformation movement, under which Western Europe's formerly united Christian community gave way to new, centralised, absolute monarchical rule, standing against the papacy and appropriating church wealth. Since that time, the British people have appeared to want a prophetic church and Christian values to stand at the heart of politics, but in fact have tried to 'manage' the country's Christian apparatus, rather than provide a home for a united church which can speak out clearly and forcibly on major issues. For effective action, believers have to distance themselves from contemporary church bureaucracy and stand alone as prophetic voices.

Currently, the field is clear for secularists and humanists. It is almost a point of honour with them that their lead on controversial subjects should destabilise Christian belief and witness. In response, the Christian churches have wheeled out their own church experts without first asking the opinion of their congregations.

Unhappily, today's politicians will only support Christian beliefs up to a point. Secularism is now so strong that it takes enormous courage for a man or woman to speak out on a major moral issue. Even this level of commitment can be made less effective by opportunists who seek to put Christianity on an equal footing with other religions.

Gladstone

Perhaps another William Gladstone (1809-1898) would be a fit leader for today's moral crusade. As Prime Minister, Gladstone had a unique vision which made him able to offer a caring outlook based on moral principles. He brought in reforms such as the disestablishment of the Church of Ireland, the Irish Land Act, the abolition of religious entrance tests in universities, elementary education and the ballot vote. All this was achieved by Gladstone alone.

Gladstone himself wanted to take holy orders, but was frustrated by his ambitious father (as was the anti-slavery campaigner William Wilberforce), who insisted that he follow him into the political field. Brought up in an evangelical context, Gladstone was later won over to High Church doctrines, and in 1838 published *The State and its relation with the Church*. In 1840, he published another book which argued in favour of the visibility of the Church of England, the certainty of the Apostolic succession, and the efficacy of the sacraments.

In 1854, Gladstone supported Archdeacon Denison who was prosecuted for preaching the Real Presence, reflecting his belief that the body and blood of Christ were actually present in the sacraments on the altar at communion. This belief contrasted strongly with that of others, who maintained that the body and blood are present only figuratively or symbolically. Gladstone's decision to support Denison was highly significant in view of his work as a politician. He was always concerned for the progress of the established church and in 1886 he went so far as to plead in a letter to a certain Cardinal Rempollo for the recognition of Anglican priestly order by the Catholic Church.

Gladstone's personal life reflected his strong faith, and he was happy for the public to know that he was a weekly communicant and a man of frugal habits, particularly in matters of sleep and food. What effect would such a prime minister have on today's media? Would his life style be seen as 'politically correct'? Doubtless, after an initial period of shock, the newspapers would begin to question whether the accounts were true, and Gladstone's hardest task would be to resist media interest in his personal life. But his keen and sympathetic interest in theology and ecclesiastical affairs would be backed up by his personal faith.

Today, the voices of Gladstone's followers are unlikely to find any listeners. Without men like Gladstone to lead the nation, there is now a distrust of those in authority, and the power of sin and evil in the human condition has increased. Politicians today find that it does not pay to be dogmatic on principle, and yet history shows that a caring disposition needs to be based on moral convictions sustained by inherited and proven law.

Can late twentieth-century society produce a politician of this calibre, one with a wholehearted faith who could resist the strongly feminist thrust which is having such a devastating effect on family life?

Where does the Government's responsibility lie?

It is all too easy to place the responsibility for action with the Government, and to wait for the Prime Minister to make public statements on the most trivial issues. Yet the general public has its own duty to encourage an ordered and Christian society.

As automation increases, surely the need for education should be re-examined to combat the danger of idleness breeding fear among those who govern? People need more than theories about the right use of leisure and the value of crafts. There is now an urgent need for support for a united Church of Christ, which can resist the Government's deliberately materialistic approach to living. Yet the conflict between the Church and materialism has made politicians wary of involvement with church affairs. Somehow, state legislation has become divorced from Christian principles. Economic progress has won the battle against Christian values.

But can economic progress really be seen as an end in itself? What is it for? What kind of a society are we aiming for? Is it still possible to persuade politicians that everything they do should be for the greater glory of God, or is that an impossible ideal?

Even among the Christian community, wealth and the acquisition of wealth are now being incorporated into regular worship. Yet although wealth can be used for God's glory, it must be put towards causes of which God approves. He has shown us the way through the example of His Son, Jesus Christ. Christians need to ask their politicians to believe in humanity's spiritual being, and in the true enrichment of human personality. Those

40

who believe in Christ's redemption need to challenge politicians to make modifications to the social structure, to plan and re-distribute wealth, to reorganise industry so that there can be global peace.

Government policies cannot change human characters, but they can control some of the forces that prey on them. Governments have the power to guide a society in which the innate goodness of human nature is given a better chance of developing and in which the preaching of the Gospel has an opportunity to deliver humanity from its fallen nature.

In the pre-Reformation era, there was an endless struggle between the opposing forces of good and evil. People found their daily lives hard and aggressive and lacked the modern scientific achievements that are taken for granted in the twentiethcentury. There was no formal distinction between Catholics and Protestants. Western Europe was totally Catholic, united by the inheritance of belief and the hope that the Gospel would be universally believed. Yet this strong religious tradition and authority did not hold. The unity came to an end with the launch of the Lutheran movement, which began when Martin Luther (1483-1540) rebelled against papal authority. He attacked the use of indulgences to raise funds for the rebuilding of St Peter's in Rome, and engaged in furious controversies with political and religious opponents. Reflecting on his actions today, one wonders if they were absolutely necessary. But his rebellion was spurred by a breakdown of trust – a situation which parallels that of the twentieth century.

Sir Thomas More (1478-1535) saw the tragedy which was unfolding before his eyes and struggled to prevent it. Who knows, his actions may yet heal the wounds of centuries? It is curious to us that More studied the same books as those whom we recognise as contemporary Protestants. Yet Cranmer, Latimer, Luther and Erasmus were all Catholics originally. Thomas More shared many of their inspirations and doubts, and yet they went in totally different directions. While Luther was to join Augustinian noviciate, More left the Carthusians at Charterhouse in the City of London in order to marry. More might well agree with T S Elliot, who said of the splintered

Christian Church: 'It would be very poor statesmanship indeed to envisage any reunion which should not fall ultimately within a scheme for complete reunion.'

Although Sir Thomas More entered Parliament and rose to be Lord Chancellor of England, he, like William Gladstone, was a man of overwhelming faith. When he finally decided he was not called to celibacy, he married without abandoning his strict rule of life and religious practices. Modern-day politicians would do well to read his *Utopia* in which he describes an ideal community which lives according to natural law and practises a natural faith. But would they, like him, be prepared to take a stand on principle, even if that might result in a death sentence? Now the loss of reputation and political allies would be the modern-day equivalent to the death sentence faced by More. If More were alive today, he would be horrified at the disunity of the Christian churches. In his world, the whole of Western Europe thought as one in terms of Christian faith, especially in relation to marriage and family life.

If the ruling authorities were to study Thomas More's *Utopia*, they would probably laugh at his old-fashioned language and grudgingly admit that he had a point, but they would doubtless overlook his vocation as a father which is evident from accounts of his life. Although the whole of More's life was centred on God, his chief purpose in life was his duty towards his four children. His books, home, career, friends, even money came second to what he believed could show the road to salvation to onlookers – his family.

In all that one reads about Thomas More, the warmth of his home and his close relationship with his children is tangible. Surely here is a lesson for us all? We might be scandalised by the fact that he married for the second time only three weeks after burying his wife who had died in childbirth, but it is clear that in a dangerous age, he was trying to safeguard his family. He honoured his second wife by marrying her, rather than taking advantage of a passing woman who might fit the bill as casual labour.

Today, all Christians are tempted to stay neutral, take no risks and steer clear of the examples of Thomas More and William

Gladstone, who were so concerned for moral standards within family life. This is particularly the case for politicians. It is always tempting to stray from the path of duty, whether it is to our family, friends, town or country, just so long as we avoid the reproaches of other people. But how long can we stay neutral? The population has a Christian inheritance of belief and unity which it must exercise as the region works once more towards a federal Europe. If we want to see Judeo-Christian values at the centre of policy-making, we must put our relationships in a Christian context.

If governments want order in present-day society, they must first seek the help of the Christian churches. Yet there is an unwillingness to take this step. Modern society wants a unified religion which denies the unique role of the crucified Christ to redeem the whole of mankind. Nevertheless, the Christian churches have a deep understanding of Man's destiny and a unique perceptive on the historical influences of our Christian inheritance.

Christ called us to be one. Although this was achieved for several centuries within Europe, dissent brought the Reformation and disintegration. Throughout the turmoil of the Reformation, society was sustained by its unflinching belief in God. Today, however, there is continuous discussion about whether the Trinitarian God exists or not. In such a confused climate, it is surely the duty of the government, let alone Christian organisations, to help nations towards a renewal of their faith and so restore order to society? The alternative is to abandon altogether our Judeo-Christian inheritance.

6

The Hippocratic tradition and the Incarnation

More thoughts on Hippocrates

To most people, Hippocrates (460-357 BC) is the founder of scientific medicine. In fact, his name is put to a group of 70 works called *The Corpus Hippocraticum.* They deal with all subjects of medicine, including prognostics, dietetics, surgery, pharmacology, health and disease, and they encompass widely differing attitudes to medicine. There is no single book whose authenticity was not already disputed in antiquity. Only fractions have been confirmed as Hippocrates' work, and even these are held in doubt. Yet the name of Hippocrates lives on.

There is a constant debate over whether Hippocrates should be viewed primarily as a philosopher or merely a practitioner. There is a stream of thought which suggests that when his writings arrived in Alexandria, they represented the remnants of medical literature which had been circulating in the fourth and fifth centuries before Christ, usually written by anonymous authors, as was the custom for technical literature of the time.

What sort of a man was Hippocrates? He was born on the island of Kos, one of the Dodecanese in the Aegean Sea. Aulus Cornelius Celsus, a Roman born in the time of Tiberius (14-37 AD) who compiled an encyclopedia on Greek medicine, calls him the first person to separate medicine from philosophy. This is revealing: Hippocrates is known to be a contemporary of Socrates, who has become known as the inspiration of modern philosophy and logic. He practised medicine on the island of

Kos, which was the centre of medical training in Ancient Greece. He travelled widely, and his death was recorded at Larisa, a city of Thessaly, 575 kilometres away from Kos.

According to Plato, Hippocrates thought of the human body as a living organism. He saw medical practice as being based on knowledge drawn from medical and philosophical research which covered a broad range of disciplines and which he tried to incorporate into one concept. He was convinced that any understanding of the body was impossible without studying it from every point of view.

Why did Hippocrates have such a huge influence? Somehow, his outlook reflects the intimate and complex relationship between a physician and his patient which demands something more than the mere ability to label and treat diseases. It is clear, too, that Hippocrates was a natural teacher. This explains his constant travelling, and might account for Kos' reputation in Ancient Greece as a centre of medical training.

Hippocrates also provided a philosophy of medicine which would give a doctor an understanding of the underlying aims and nature of medicine, and the nature of health and disease. He taught that a physician could not work in isolation from other disciplines, and this is something which is missing from medical practice today.

What should we value in Ancient Greece's medical practice?

The Greeks would no doubt be highly disapproving of contemporary medicine. They believed that all natural forces emanated from the divinity of their gods, and would no doubt find it hard to marry this belief to today's experimental science, test-tube dramas, and the concept of the human body as a mere machine.

Yet then, as now, medicine was the science of preventing, diagnosing, alleviating or curing physical and mental disease, and the search for any substance which could be used to treat disease. The main difference today lies in the introduction of synthetic drugs, and an increasing reliance on drugs and sophisticated surgical techniques.

In ancient practice, the science of medicine was overlaid with magic, rites and beliefs. Despite this, diet and exercise was advocated even then as a means of maintaining health and warding off illness. The physician had a duty to observe his patients' life styles so that he could pinpoint the likely cause of a particular illness.

The body was understood to be made up of four main fluids: blood, phlegm, yellow bile and black bile. If the supply of these fluids became unbalanced, the result was illness, which could only be treated by restoring the balance. Illness was seen as a crisis, and patients were encouraged to seek rest and quiet, and advised to embark on elaborate rituals based on dietetics. This approach was used for centuries to treat cases that did not require surgery.

By modern standards, ancient medical practices seem random. Yet Greek archaeological sites reflect a sophistication which can be all too easily dismissed. The Romans enhanced Greek achievements with their aqueducts, water-supplies and drainage systems. Systematic excavations at Pompeii, which was destroyed by a volcanic eruption in 63 AD, have revealed a complex network of surgeries and nursing homes which support this understanding.

Behind ancient medicine lay a strongly held belief that people must accept and prepare for death. Although the Greeks did not believe in one God, historical and archaeological evidence reveals their strong religious convictions and their belief in divine powers which could protect and be beneficial in themselves. Life may have been violent and often extremely dangerous, yet they spent time and effort embellishing sanctuaries, such as Delphi, home of the famous oracle. These efforts were supported by personal votive offerings and the wearing of amulets to ward off evil.

A cult rose up around the god Asclepius, who was seen as a hero and god of healing. Magnificent temples were erected in his honour. People seeking cures had to go through an incubation period and adhere to a dietetic regimen. Later, baths (including

46

those at Pergamum where there were radioactive springs), gymnasia, even theatres were built at these centres, making them seem more like sanatoria. The cult of Asclepius had its roots in Thessaly, and was well-known to Hippocrates, who died nearby. It is clear that although Hippocrates' followers were highly organised when it came to realising their medical calling, they needed Asclepius to enhance their spiritual calling.

The Hippocratic Oath begins with the words: "I swear by Apollo the physician and Asclepius, and Health and all-Heal and all the gods and goddesses, that according to my ability and judgement, I will keep this Oath . . ." Later, the oath goes on: "I will give no deadly medicine to anyone if asked, nor suggest any such counsel; and in like manner I will not give to a woman a pessary to produce abortion . . . With purity and with holiness I will pass my life and practice of my Art. But should I trespass and violate this Oath, may the reverse be my lot."

These words are awe-inspiring, particularly in the twentieth century, when the child in the womb is often held of little account. Surely it is time for contemporary society to give serious thought to a code of ethics which holds steadfast to a moral obligation.

The spectacular career of Galen of Pergamum shows the impact of an ethical outlook on medical practice. He started life as a gladiator physician, tending to prisoners of war or condemned criminals who fought to the death in the amphitheatres, and rose to be court physician to Marcus Aurelius. He excelled in diagnosis and prognosis, besides being known for careful analysis as an anatomist and physiologist. Later he laid the foundations of pharmacological thought and practices for centuries to come. Yet in spite of his enormous experience of death and disease, he held fast to his belief in a final purpose and to his religious outlook. Even the most complex dissections gave him cause to praise and thank God.

Could these historical figures have a role in the debate about modern medicine? There is an important thread running through all current discussion about medical ethics: it is always separated from religious belief. This trend continues in the late twentieth-century. Most people recognise that evil is not just the absence of good, nor do they see it as a purely random tendency in an individual who wants to pursue his or her own ends. Evil affects flesh, body and soul and the whole outlook on life. Those who adhere to a Christian belief have to accept that evil is present everywhere in the world, and that it is organised, co-ordinated and at times concentrated. It is actively opposed to the will of God, but although it sometimes seems to have the upper hand, it is ultimately subject to His power. This awareness distinguished and enriched ancient medicine, but is absent from modern-day medical practice.

Those who have worked to help and advise mothers seeking abortion are only too aware of the number of nurses who give birth to unplanned children. The code of ethics which used to protect the medical fraternity has all too clearly broken down. Family life now survives on a day-to-day basis, and the same applies to the doctor/patient relationship. The mutual respect, communication and shared decisions which used to strengthen family life and the dignity of women have disappeared.

The family unit offers peace to the greater family of humankind, yet family members are now confronted with a range of conflicting outlooks on their physical well-being which can be frightening and even overwhelming. A re-reading of humanity's medical history offers some perspective and comfort.

Doctors and the Incarnation

There is no doubt that flourishing scientific research has produced startling changes of outlook in the field of medicine. It now poses a possible challenge to Christian belief as it probes every aspect of human development. If the word 'Incarnation' crops up in conversation with physicians, it is likely to be greeted with a heavy silence. How can we convince sceptical doctors that God the Father became incarnate through the submission of his mother to the Word of God? Motherhood surely holds the key to this mystery and to new life. Yet is it possible even to discuss the vexed question of the virgin birth in the context of modern biological science?

Many people follow Jesus in a fairly uninstructed way and try to observe their faith by following an ill-defined moral code. The inherited tradition of Mosaic law, the Ten Commandments, which constitute an organic body of religious and moral ideals, tends to be avoided. Based on the Hebrew concept of God, these clear and succinct rules are widely recognised as representing an ethos which could be called the common property of humanity. But are even these commandments enough, when God asks us for a total commitment? Must we carry on resisting and finding excuses as we try to rationalise our own desires alongside the reality of conceiving, carrying and bearing a child? Will there ever be an acknowledgement once more of the holiness of the womb and the uniqueness of the order of creation within God's world?

In obstetrics, it is almost impossible to introduce the concept of the womb as a holy place and the seat of creation. Pregnancy is now weighed up against a sliding scale of values. It is therefore not surprising that many women decide against continuing a pregnancy if anything is wrong with the foetus following a course of intense technical data.

Gynaecologists are often accused of 'playing God'. In fact, their criteria for advising abortion are often based on concerns for maternal or foetal health and 'quality of life'. Even so, theirs is a very imperfect system of choice. When an abortion is performed legally, often on social grounds, the decision is not defended as 'morally correct', but rather the best possible alternative in a fallen world. Unhappily, the selective destruction of millions of babies who are thought to be socially 'at risk' cannot increase respect for life among the population. Abortion must by its very nature be understood as a social evil.

The extraordinary organ called the placenta, which unites the mammalian foetus to the maternal uterus and serves as its means of nutrition and excretion, is the best illustration of the holiness of conception. When studying its functions – still so imperfectly understood, despite the advances of medical knowledge – it is awe-inspiring to see this organ, which ensures the birth of future generations, functioning so perfectly. Yet the human placenta has its counterparts in other forms of animal life. The uniqueness of

49

a human being is his ability to relate to God, rather than purely to his biological make-up.

Few people appreciate the significance of the role played by the placenta, through which a developing child in the womb is nourished by its mother. Little is known of its detailed physiology because the placenta is a difficult organ to study. It lasts only the duration of the pregnancy and then degenerates once it is detached and expelled from the womb after the birth. Yet before birth, it acts as the foetus' lungs, intestines and kidneys, while transferring waste matter into the mother's circulation and taking in food and oxygen.

The blood runs from the foetus through the umbilical cord (which connects the placenta with the foetus) to spread out in the foetal side of the placenta. It is always separated from the mother's blood on the maternal side of the placenta by the placental membrane. Only a few diseases, such as syphilis and rubella, can pass this membrane to affect the child.

It is important to give some thought to the human blood system which develops in the womb. The developing child is genetically distinct from the mother from the moment of conception. It has a separate physical system that operates totally independently from the mother. So, from a biological standpoint, the mother provides sources of nutrients so that the embryo or zygote can develop and differentiate to its genetic capacity. It is the unique gift of women that they can reflect in their wombs God's gift of creation.

In the Christian Eucharist the believer receives the body and blood of Christ. The wonder of priesthood is seen in the male, and is the counterpart to the demands made by God on women. There is no attempt by the Roman Catholic Church to deny the presence of Christ in the bread and wine which are offered at communion, but there is a strong movement in other Christian bodies to deny this. This resistance to the miracle of Holy Communion often acts as a bar to a greater understanding of the Eucharist. Yet the churches are in general united by a collective and widely-held view that the Eucharist is a sacrifice and a constant reminder of Christ's sacrifice for humanity that will lead to redemption.

The calling exercised by parenthood needs to be considered alongside the sacrificial role of priesthood. Parenthood necessarily involves a sacrificial outlook. An even greater sacrifice is demanded of women who are called to be mothers and men who are called to the priesthood. It is not for nothing that mothers are described as 'tiger-like', while the call of priesthood has a depth that often cannot be combined with that of biological parenthood.

At the time of the Reformation, there was much argument about the issue of transubstantiation, or whether the bread and wine truly became the body and blood of Christ at the Eucharist. Little, if any, credence was given to the idea that people should see a greater understanding of creation and the role of women within it. Now, with the world-wide acceptance of abortion. Christians need to be awake to the reality of what is happening, and the challenge that abortion poses to the incarnate Word.

A medical friend reflected in her daily life her love of people and the unborn. People like her deserve sympathy, for they are dealing constantly with life and death and must always work to reconcile the demands made on them with their consciences. She, knowing my concern on this matter once said: "Transubstantiation, to me, is both biologically and theologically incomprehensible. I cannot imagine how the bread and wine, even if microscopically examined, could be anything other than bread and wine. Christ died for my sins and those of all who confess Him as Saviour. There is no need for any further sacrifice and if there was, His sacrifice would be discredited. What we do in church (or at home) is in memory of that sacrifice. This must be a standard Biblical anniversary. The claims for a real sacrifice sound medieval and are an abuse of power."

These words should prompt us to turn to the example of Mary, the mother of Jesus Christ. The miracle of the holiness and uniqueness of creation is embodied in her, and stands as an example for the whole of humanity. We should also be aware that since the sixteenth century much attention has been paid to the Eucharistic sacrifice in all parts of western Christendom, and seek to understand that although sacrifice, usually of birds and animals, has always featured in religions, the Eucharistic sacrifice was the first to put an emphasis on life and prayer.

Blood is fundamental to life, and doctors and scientists know only too well that chemical determination and analysis of the blood is essential for an accurate picture of the health or otherwise of the individual. Blood acts to transport oxygen and to remove carbon dioxide from the cells; to carry food substances to the cells and remove waste matter; to remove excess heat and carry it to the surface of the body; to control many vital processes by the transport of hormones and other chemical substances; and finally to defend the body against infection by the transport of antitoxins, antibodies and white blood cells to the infected part.

All this activity is begun in a foetus or developing child and must be understood as a repetitive cycle which occurs down the generations. The typical reaction to the Biblical phrase, 'Go forth and multiply and fill the earth' tends to be one of amusement (Genesis 9:7). Nevertheless God wants to see the continuation of human life, and Scripture acknowledges that children are a gift from God.

In the late twentieth-century, childbearing is regarded as a feminine right, with scientific medicine there to satisfy our demands for children in case of infertility. The widespread introduction of artificial contraception was initially opposed by the church, but today family planning is the norm among Christians and non-Christians, both in and outside marriage. Nevertheless, the provision of birth control to the unmarried, and especially to teenagers, whose bodies are still maturing, is questionable.

In fact, society has changed radically in a relatively short space of time. Rather than wringing our hands, we need to study our theological, medical and social history and find out how women's physical well-being has been affected through the years.

It is easy to forget that Jesus experienced all the developments within Mary's womb which are normal for a human foetus. But the miracle of the Incarnation should reassure Christians of the value which God places on humanity. Life, like death, is an emotive word, especially when the majority does not believe in any after-life.

Jesus taught his followers to love God and to love their neighbours as they loved themselves. That injunction applies as much to the child in the womb as it does to the rest of humanity. The Incarnation offers hope to humankind, but also acts as a rebuke to those who fail to respect human life and to a society which has moved away from God.

The Hippocratic Oath forbade doctors to give women any abortive suppository. Yet even then, some doctors defied the oath, and infanticide and exposure of children has spurred the drafting of new legislation from the earliest times. In the early eighth century, Roman law decreed that all male children and first born female children must be reared, and ruled that no other child should be killed unless it was crippled or deformed at birth. Even these children had to be shown to five neighbours to obtain their sanction before they could be exposed. Any new-born child was recognised as a separate identity and was legally entitled to a funeral. Within the Hippocratic tradition, children were permitted the right to be born and were acknowledged as separate human identities.

Would it be possible for today's society to accept the challenge posed by the Hippocratic Oath and to allow all conceptions to lead to a birth, particularly when so many people want to adopt? Should we not listen more closely to the Word of God, who chose to become incarnate through the womb of Mary, and so directed Christians at all times to respect human life in the uterus? There are many arguments against abortion, and this is one of them. An argument which is all too often overlooked is the one warning of the consequences of abortion. If abortion is wrong, one would expect it to have harmful effects. The fact that these harmful effects have clearly materialised could speak more powerfully to our generation than theological arguments. One likely result of this, however, is that Christians are less likely to go into medicine. Unless the Christian public creates a demand for doctors and nurses who have ethical values in line with their own, such people will not enter the medical profession.

7

Ideals and their critics

Who has ideals?

The ideal of the philosopher/physician flourished during the Renaissance. A doctorate in the arts was seen as a natural stepping stone to a career in medicine, while the route to a medical chair used to be through a teaching post in philosophy or logic. In sixteenth-century England, the Hippocratic Oath was most frequently printed in four distinct translations with commentaries, omissions and additions. The Hippocratic ideals represented the sixteenth-century doctor's model.

Every generation since Hippocrates has tried valiantly to aspire to similar ideals. In the twentieth century, naturally idealistic teenagers are swayed by radio, television, newspapers and the cinema, but how can they relate to medical ethics?

As a carpenter, Our Lord learnt the basics of His trade, along with a phenomenal knowledge of the Old Testament books and their ideals. He would have known the name and purpose of every tool in His workshop and an understanding of the different types of wood. He expects no less of his followers. Every Christian must accept a duty to bear witness both inside and outside the Church.

Although few would choose the role of leader, Christians have to acknowledge the divine and supernatural nature of God in order to be true children of God. But how can they do so at a time of unprecedented social upheaval?

Sir Thomas More (1478-1535) offers a shining example of

Christian witness. Many of the problems which confront today's society have their parallels in the turbulent society of Tudor England. His ideals sustained a purity and virtuous way of life which overcame all the court gossip, but could not prevent his execution on Tower Hill. He had been accused of high treason because he had opposed the Act of Supremacy which confirmed Henry VIII and his successors with the title of 'the only supreme head on earth of the Church of England'.

This took place at a time when a disturbed Europe faced the Reformation. Even so, society was only beginning to divide into Protestant or Roman Catholic factions, and remained united in a common Christian faith. Thomas More was a genuine reformer and an enemy of all forms of superstition, showing a personal order based on Christian ideals which promoted a right use of leisure, the value of crafts, the danger of idleness and the importance of education if channelled in the right direction. All this was expounded in his book *Utopia,* along with an awareness of death. He has been criticised for the latter – but it was probably a result of his Carthusian training. It may even have been a premonition of the events which would lead his friend, a Catholic king who had lost his own ideals, to martyr him.

More's London had an international feel, as it does today. But it differed from the London we know in that it was based on the Thames, where ships from all parts of the world discharged their wares among an abundance of pageants, scandals, riots and vigorous activity. The system was essentially patriarchal in its style of government and there was a well-established system of apprenticeship, aldermen and guilds. Signs of decay were already apparent in the new and more frivolous life which developed under Henry Tudor. More was fortunate in that he came from a well-established city family. His father was an eminent lawyer and judge, and this background made it possible for him to become a member of the household of Archbishop Morton. This led him to study classics at Oxford University and then to study law at his father's request. Later he was called to the bar and became a lecturer at Furnival's Inn.

There is some uncertainty over when More tested his calling with the Carthusians at the London Charterhouse, but he was deeply attracted by the monastic life, and lived with them for as much as four years. This was a turning point in More's personal life, and may well have been the period when he developed such strong personal ideals relating to family life.

The monastic foundation of the London Charterhouse was dedicated to the Annunciation of the Virgin Mary, and was commonly known as the House of the Salutation of the Mother of God. Many people are puzzled by his association with the monastic order: More took no vows and was not even a novice. There is no record of his life within the Charterhouse. It was not unusual for a monastic foundation to offer hospitality for months on end to young men pursuing their own occupations, but somehow historians sense something different here. Certainly, More's personal life revealed an intense inner core, based on profound prayer which dominated his thoughts and actions.

The Carthusian movement has a profound devotion to Mary, the Mother of God. Even if More abandoned the idea of joining them, he did not abandon his devotion to Mary as his ideal of perfect motherhood. Although he is said to have had no profound religious experiences, a personal friend of More's, Reginald Pole, reveals that a period of great doubt was dispersed by 'a light supernatural and a supernatural love given him by the mercy of God'. This must go some way to explain a man who had a genuine desire for an austere and solitary life, and yet had a brilliant public career which showed clarity of vision, contentment and realism.

More's home at Chelsea, where he lived with his wife and children, became a centre of intellectual life and was his alternative to the Carthusians' contemplative way of life. Here, he lived his intense personal life of prayer and devoted his time, love and energy to his children. Somehow his books, career, friends and money were of little importance compared to this home and family. More's activities and outlook are largely reflected in *Utopia*, a book which revealed his own deep spiritual convictions wrapped in a pagan guise.

Was More given a special mission by God to guide people to see the ideals which can be found in family life if based on prayer and love? Does his execution mean that he failed?

Subsequent centuries have shown that we have preferred to concentrate on the Reformation rather than look to Thomas More and his astonishing approach to life. Although he was undoubtedly a mystic, his life in the secular world alongside his life as a husband and father fills one with awe.

Today, we are once again faced with a deep unrest, when authority in civil and Christian administration is being challenged at every level. We need to look once again at this man who met an equivalent challenge in a hard and aggressive age.

The influence of the Wolfenden Report

These days, it is customary to hand problematic issues over to 'experts' whom we trust first to establish and then to achieve what we want. This is how we avoid looking at moral dilemmas in any depth. The result – which would certainly not have appealed to Sir Thomas More – is a liberal interpretation of the law, which gives an equal hearing to all views. Most people, however, realise that the majority view is not always appropriate, and want the law to be subjected to rigorous scrutiny so that it reflects a moral basis.

Up to very recently, English law reflected Christian standards, and was drafted by people who were, in the main, Christian. As a result, the English tend to assume that the country's civil law does indeed rest on a firm moral code. But the Wolfenden Report of 1951 showed that this was not the case.

The Report was chaired by Lord Wolfenden (1906-1985) when a Royal Commission was ordered in 1951 to investigate homosexuality and prostitution. It recommended legalising homosexual acts between consenting adults in private. Shortly after the report was completed, its recommendations were enacted by law. Many people link the report with an acceleration of the slide towards the moral maze of the late twentieth century.

Homosexuality and prostitution are by no means new phenomena. Plato and Socrates both extolled love between two males as superior to heterosexual relationships. However, even in Ancient Rome there was a strong tradition of family life. In

Jewish culture, the importance of family life was (and remains) paramount, and there were heavy penalties imposed on those who threatened it.

Today, many gay movements want to affirm the homosexual life style, but this outlook rejects the family structure as the basis of society. Yet the basis of family structure is unvarying, for it stems from an intensively creative natural order. Nowhere is this more apparent than in the field of abortion. Despite all the reassurances of doctors, lobbying groups and politicians, people are generally well-aware that legalised abortion has resulted in the killing of viable children in the womb.

The situation has reached crisis point, and some people are even prepared to kill doctors who carry out abortions. One man in America who actually went this far has been threatened with the electric chair.

The Christian churches do all they can to defend the life of the child in the womb, but after so many years of protesting with little effect, they have become passive. At Christian book shops of most denominations, pro-life books have been quietly withdrawn, or the enquirer is advised to look under 'pastoral care'. Most people are quite unable now to support publicly a child's right to life, let alone accept that abortion strikes at the entire moral order and at the core of family life.

Few people would deny that human life in the womb is precious. It is a gift from God, whose love is infinite. It is a hard view to hold onto, however, when we know that our monthly mortgage payments now take priority over the unplanned conception of a child.

A former US president, Thomas Jefferson, said in 1809: 'The care of human life and happiness and not their destruction is the just and only legitimate object of good government.' Even this statement is challenged when it is extended to include the child in the womb. When Jefferson was alive there was a strict moral control, and the widespread practice of abortion which America, the United Kingdom and other countries face today, did not exist.

If we could collectively accept that all life begins at conception, society would have a greater sense of order. But this is not the case, and nowhere is this more apparent than in the medical profession. Many Christian doctors struggle to reach a consensus about when an abortion is justified, and yet in practice they find that each case is unique. They all agree that the present situation is far from satisfactory.

Human life, like all biological life, is biologically a continuum marked by certain stages. Conception and gestation consists of fertilisation, implantation, primitive streak, development of heart and blood circulation, quickening, followed by viability as an independent human being and birth. No doctor would hesitate to remove a live foetus implanted in the Fallopian tube (known as an ectopic pregnancy) because this condition endangers the life of the mother. They would also generally be prepared to fit an inter-uterine device that may allow fertilisation but would prevent implantation.

Christian doctors know that they have to accept responsibility before God as His agents in creation, and this can lead to difficult choices. They may find themselves having to remove a live foetus from a uterus because of a bleeding ovarian tumour. Such situations pose important questions for expectant mothers and those who care for them. Doctors faced with these choices often feel they need rules that will protect them from the pressure of expectations that they should 'help' or 'conform'. One of the most wretched experiences for a Christian general practitioner is to be confronted by a girl who has unintentionally become pregnant and who is under intense pressure to conform with the wishes of her parents or society in general and have an abortion. Doctors and patients would be protected in such situations if the law firmly vetoed such social abortions.

The state takes great pride in the fact that it takes responsibility for the families of soldiers who have died in defence of their country. Yet the authorities cannot accept the implications of being in any way responsible for the many thousands of potentially healthy children who are aborted for social reasons. They support the practice of abortion, but are unlikely to admit publicly that abortion is a powerful deterrent to a possible population explosion.

In the 1960s, the world witnessed an explosion in the use of contraceptives. In the 1990s we are seeing that contraceptives have failed us. But it remains hard to accept that the combined contraceptive pill which was hailed as the greatest advance of women's rights this century has failed to realise its early promise.

Artificial contraceptives have given women sexual licence, but they have left many gravely confused about what it means to be a woman. Why? Because women, while having unlimited access to abortion and contraceptive advice, are equally dismayed at the grave consequences for their wombs and ability to conceive. This can in turn lead to a rejection of the value of being a woman and a desire for equality with men.

It is surely time for the British Medical Association to make an honest and circumspect statement clarifying its attitude to abortion and affirming its commitment, as a doctors' association, to save life. Of all professions, doctors enter the medical field with high ideals. I am convinced that they have an awareness of right and wrong and of the natural law. In other words, they have a conscience and a fundamental ability to appreciate the value of human life.

Unfortunately, human life is now generally judged by its usefulness to society. From time to time, the general public is thrilled to read of anonymous children who are flown half way round the world to receive the latest life-saving treatment at huge expense. The great skill and kindness of the attending consultants is noted with appreciation. Such cases test doctors' sense of right and wrong. Just as some consciences can become blunted, and wills to protect life can vacillate, so God's view of human life can be ignored by the laws of the prevailing governments.

To God, humankind is inherently precious, because it is made in His image. God longs for all men and women to reconcile themselves to Him. These are not just words. Full reconciliation requires the recognition of the Incarnation and the fact that God came to us in human form. People need to understand that belief in the Incarnation is not in itself an ideology, a creed or even a party allegiance. God expressed His love for us in a most profound sanctity when He surrendered Himself to a woman's womb. He was only able to do this with the full co-operation of Mary, who was ready to do God's will, whatever the danger. She did not refuse motherhood despite living in a society which

60

treated unmarried mothers with great harshness. Instead, she accepted His challenge gladly and openly as part of God's plan for the world. She did not deny God's will.

Today, women are paying a high price for their ignorance. But to what extent are they to blame? Perhaps they are on the receiving end of one of the greatest confidence tricks that the world has ever known. World population experts and manufacturers of contraceptives, let alone those who run abortion clinics, must be seen as influential in playing down the effects of abortion and the real impact of the possible side effects, and in keeping law suits at bay. The main risk of steroid contraceptives is in encouraging a change in behaviour – resulting from the false belief that sex is safe, provided pregnancy is prevented. In fact, business tycoons have made a fortune out of budding sexual awareness.

The effects are now being felt by society, and it is now not unusual to hear of women who have died after a short and acute illness, leaving young children to be brought up by their father or other relatives. Blame can be assigned to all sorts of people or circumstances in this situation. But perhaps one of the reasons for this increasing tendency is the enormous freedom now accorded to the mothers of young children.

Under current legislation in the United Kingdom, men and women are totally equal, regardless of many women's roles as wives and mothers. Many mothers have gone along with this outlook, and have tried to juggle a career, a marriage and home life. The husbands in such partnerships can often be left feeling very alone, because their wives simply have no time to support them either socially or emotionally.

Modern society's denial of God's will is now even more militant, while the outlook that describes motherhood as a sacrificial role does not fit in with the feminist movement. Throughout the centuries, motherhood has produced warmth, sensitivity, love and generosity. The source of these qualities is a mother's love for her children. That love can be endangered by the act of abortion and the use of contraceptives, if they are not channelled through the love of God. While women have unlimited access to abortion and contraception, they are often dismayed by the

61

attendant problems which are now threatening their procreative abilities.

Today's society operates on the understanding that anything which displeases can be disposed of and that people have the 'right' to do whatever they want with their own bodies – including the contents of the womb. Abortion (the taking of a human life), and artificial contraception (which prevents life from beginning), both interfere with the natural development of a woman's body.

Christians need to hold firmly to the belief that all men and women are made in the image of God. This is not a sentimental view. It is time to return once again to the ideal that a person who can carry life in the womb deserves as much respect as the developing child. We need to dispense with the outlook under which a woman has a right to decide whether to give life or death to her child. The time has come to give greater consideration to the ethics of adoption.

The ethics of adoption

Psychologists are well aware that although a woman can terminate her pregnancy, she cannot bring an end to her motherhood. Her pregnancy, however brief, brings a memory which will not go away. There is a great difference between an abortion, and giving up a child for adoption. The first cuts off a natural process in the middle of development. The second may be an agonising and bitter experience, but it is a complete process. The act of childbirth alone makes it possible to accept and put aside motherhood. The process may be accompanied by profound sorrow, but it is not accompanied by the corrosive grief which follows an abortion.

Perhaps here it is useful to address the issue of surrogate motherhood – the bearing of an unrelated embryo in the womb, either for a fee or as a voluntary act, on behalf of an infertile couple. An Israeli gynaecologist once said that he had implanted 12 post-menopausal women with embryos. All of them could refer to the developing foetus only as 'the other woman's child'.

Could it be that they were not able to offer their own motherhood for the child?

Many women do go on to give birth after unexpectedly becoming pregnant, but choose to turn away from their motherhood by giving the child up for adoption. This is why social workers sometimes advise adopted children not to seek their natural parent. An example may be particularly useful here when considering the practicalities of adoption.

I met a woman who was in the process of adopting her second child. Nobody could have wished for a more loving mother, but she was unable to conceive. The child she adopted was the fifth child of a 22-year-old woman. The mother was determined to hand over the child in person, because she was entrusting it to a woman who could give the mother-love that she could not. The courts somehow understood and gave both mothers bouquets of flowers. In this instance, the ethics of love were truly at work.

Men and women's procreative faculties entail basic principles which make them partners with God in creation. Procreation is humankind's greatest privilege and gravest responsibility. Men and women have obligations to subsequent generations, and yet modern liberal abortion laws have upset the balance by facilitating sexual indulgence.

8

The Roman inheritance:
a conflict of ideals and disorder

Most people would agree that there are many diverse moral and political opinions in today's society, all of which are held in good faith. As a result, there is a tendency to try and understand one's fellow-citizens rather than exert a Christian influence on them. In fact, when people state their belief that 'anything goes', it is now quite acceptable for those who believe otherwise to shrug their shoulders and say that it is essential for people to 'do their own thing'. Unfortunately, when such a liberal attitude is applied to law and moral values in an attempt to provide a wide basis for decision-making, even larger moral dilemmas appear.

Despite people's faith in the prevailing legal system, it is painfully obvious that the system favours abortion. Doctors and nurses who oppose abortion receive sympathy but very little else. A well-known gynaecologist once announced in public that he had reprimanded his health authority for not having performed enough abortions over a fixed period. He did not even consider the possibility that congratulations might have been in order. In one city, abortions are carried out all day, every day except Christmas Day – yet few people appreciate the irony of the situation. It seems that Christian ideology, if only in this instance, is being taken to excess.

Currently, there is a trend against enforcing morality through law, and as a result the public's faith in the judiciary has been shaken. There seem to be irreconcilable differences of opinion on all medical issues relating to the interpretation of the Abortion Act of 1967, such as amniocentesis, contraception, tests for

Down's Syndrome, donation of embryos, euthanasia and so on. People have little opportunity to reach a reflective and informed conclusion. The liberal media coverage alone is enough to fill a Christian, or indeed any member of the public, with despair. However, in Britain public involvement in research for the Warnock report offered some hope. The report, carried out in 1984, was initiated by the Tory government which was anxious about new methods of artificial conception. A committee was formed under Lady Warnock with a remit to study the recent medical advances in 'human fertilisation and embryology'. Chief and most contentious was whether human embryos should be available to medical scientists in their laboratories.

The Warnock report in turn led to the formation of a central committee to oversee the application of human fertilisation and embryology. Yet few people understand the enormity of the holocaust over which the committee presides. Its members are witnesses to the one great exception to the conventional prohibition on the co-option of human beings, however small, as experimental subjects.

Sometimes, hard choices are necessary, and the Law Lords have to make a firm decision when the law is interpreted in a way that can only be called excessive. After 4 million abortions in the UK since the Abortion Act of 1967, has that point now been reached? Has the number of women disturbed by abortion reached such a scale that the law should be reassessed?

It is time for a lively, open debate on the abortion law, allowing the public an opportunity to support interested parties for and against abortion, and to listen to their evidence. We might then be able to confront with confidence the wildly erroneous assumption that the current scale of abortion is essential for society. Pressure groups such as Life, the Society for the Protection of the Unborn Child, the Council for Civil Liberties, independent bodies based on family care, university research groups or government committees could all provide informed research which could help individuals to reach an informed decision.

In many disputes on law and order, the heat can be taken out of the debate if the protagonists realise that they are dealing with a highly emotive issue. Many wonder, quite rightly, whether any

65

rational debate is possible in the field of abortion because emotions run so high. Yet the public has a right to know the facts. There has been no debate on this issue for so long that increasingly conscience has become a matter for the individual rather than society. As a result, society as a whole is in a dilemma: when faced with debate about abortion in the media, most people find it safer to express no opinion at all, whatever the promptings of their own hearts. Although precise information will not convert everybody to a single point of view, the public does have a right to firm evidence for and against the act of abortion.

In a democracy, people are accorded the right to know how the country is run so that the Government cannot abuse its powers. Politicians have to juggle to try and overcome the tensions that arise between respect for the wishes of the majority and for those of the minority. Yet such confrontational attitudes and beliefs could be mitigated if the law was changed to allow public debate on emotive issues such as those raised by abortion. If a country's legal system is to win respect and to be reflected in the nation's morals and medical ethics, the public needs to be allowed a role in debate and possible action relating to life in the womb.

The Roman inheritance of ideals

An outstanding feature of Roman law was its international flavour, which meant it could ease differences between Romans and foreign subject states. As a result, Roman law was adopted with local modifications all over Europe.

Even the deification of dead Roman emperors served a political purpose, as it could present the emperor's family as a national ideal. One important aspect of Roman law which is too often overlooked is that it embraced a whole system of obligation arising from free debate. This was backed up by a vigorous formal and legal process which was implemented by means of solemn and inflexible codes without which the laws could not take effect. In other words, no legal reform could be made without rational argument.

A good illustration of this approach is the introduction of the *patria potestas* into the definition of marriage. Marriage was strictly monogamous, and was defined as a union of a man and woman as a lifelong relationship. Later, a social interpretation of family order became part of the Roman constitution. Here, the *pater familias* exerted a sovereign authority over all members of his family, even if his family was with *manus* (this was an informal marriage, where a man and woman lived together in the man's home for a year at a stretch). Essentially, *manus* signified the power of the husband over his wife, whether it was through a religious ceremony which was performed in the presence of ten witnesses, or by the sale of the wife to the prospective husband. The *patria potestas* gave a man complete control over his wife, sons and daughters, and even daughters-in-law and their children. He had the right to punish his household and was even permitted to kill the new-born or expose unwanted children. Twentieth-century society – probably rightly – would see him as a dictator.

It is a relief that such laws do not apply today. But the Romans did have a procedure to restrain the husband's role. This was the family council, made up of relatives and friends, who applied custom and sacred law to control the situation. It would have been difficult for an individual to advocate the killing of a child, because the family council would stand in the way. We would like to think that such caring services were available today, but they are not. In Rome, the family council protected the family to which it belonged. Such committees do not exist today.

The personhood of Christ in the Roman world

Plato (429-347 BC) a Greek philosopher and writer who believed that to understand the body, one must understand the mind and spirit also, used to pose questions on this issue. He makes some interesting comments on nature of the human soul, dividing it into three parts: the natural appetites, the spirit or resolution by which humans resist their appetites, and reason which determines when the appetites should be resisted.

Plato would probably have rejoiced if he had known the value which Jesus Christ placed on humanity. We must not lose sight of the full humanity of Jesus Christ alongside our knowledge of his parthenogenic (both human and divine) conception.

Humanity is like the gathering together of beams of light. It is the foundation of God's plan for His humanity and His unique act of salvation. So it is natural to see the Incarnation as the guarantee of the hope and reality of God's presence as He seeks to rescue humanity from sin. 'He [Christ] is the image of the unseen God, the first-born of all creation, for in him were created all things in heaven and earth: everything visible and invisible.' (Colossians 1:15,16) 'He exists before all things, and in him all things hold together.' (Colossians 1:17) Twentieth-century research challenges the reality of the Incarnation and has left society with nagging doubts and unable to accept the Word of God.

Although the gospels are concerned with the birth, life and teaching of our Lord, and contain nothing about induced abortion, people still find it difficult to accept Jesus Christ as Saviour in the knowledge of the current fate of unplanned pregnancies. It is easy to believe that personhood of a child does not start at a conception, but scientific research is proving other-wise, and it is now difficult to look for excuses even with an early abortion. Life has come in a full circle, and people want to find excuses for the modern interpretation of life in the womb: the population is suffering collectively from a profound sense of guilt. That guilt cannot be relieved by modern research. Although theological and legal concepts of life's beginnings have had to change substantially in outlook, the Incarnation – where Christ was conceived by the Holy Spirit in the womb of a virgin – remains a constant challenge which alone cannot be revised in line with modern life. No theologian can even attempt to say that Christ only became Himself after three months gestation. In fact, God ordained the Incarnation from His place in eternity. Christ's birth, life, death and resurrection were the sovereign work of God.

It is easy to feel a sense of superiority over previous genera-tions when surveying the advances in medicine and biology. Anyone claiming the uniqueness of personhood from conception is easily argued down. The fact that possibly half of all human embryos are lost in the menstrual flow prior to their implantation lends force to the argument. The development of in-vitro fertilisation has given rise to a new set of medico-legal and ethical dilemmas in this field and a new intensity of debate, yet there is still a gap of five calendar months between the age of the oldest embryo to be grown in a dish, and the youngest foetus/child of about 24 weeks' gestation who has been born alive.

The book of Ecclesiasticus has some sage advice for medical researchers in the twentieth century: 'As you do not know the path of the wind or how the body is formed in the mother's womb, so you cannot understand the work of God, the Maker of all things.' (Ecclesiastes 11:5) Is humanity meant to understand the mysteries of life? Are people prepared to accept that the ultimate in human achievement is to form a relationship with our creator God?

It is worth taking a look at Herod, King of the Jews (37-4 BC), at the time of Christ's birth, whose ruthlessness won peace for 37 years in a country which was very hard to rule. Although in the last resort he was answerable to Rome, he enjoyed sufficient independence and personal prestige to make his mark on history. Somehow, he seemed to know that he was living in a time of apocalyptic religious ferment, and he was quick to use any supernatural signs to his advantage, such as the coming of the Magi. There were many such signs in the course of his reign, and the story of the Magi and the plans of Herod are woven together so closely that it is hard to extricate them from each other. There were many similar links made with the supernatural at the time. At the time of the birth of the Emperor Augustus, for example, a report on the oracle by Suetonius led to a decision by the Roman Senate that no one born that year should be allowed to live.

The men known as Magi were originally a class of priests from Hedes in Egypt, but at the time of the birth of Christ, they were men who came from the East who possessed profound astrological and astronomical wisdom.

The star which the wise men followed has often been used as a means of dating the birth of Jesus, but St Ignatius (85-107 AD) offers a deeper interpretation of the star and the coming of the

69

Magi. According to him, the coming of Christ destroyed all necromancy and magic, as represented by the Magi. St Paul appears to support this view: 'So you are no longer aliens or foreign visitors; you are fellow citizens with the holy people of God and part of God's household, you are built on the foundations of the apostles and prophets, and Christ Jesus himself is the cornerstone.' (Ephesians 2: 19,20) In other words, St Paul saw a completely new world developing.

It is time now to consider the Holy Innocents, the children of Bethlehem who were massacred by Herod the Great in a vain attempt to destroy the infant Jesus. All of these little children were clearly greatly loved: they were born into a strongly-held tradition which valued life at birth. They ranged in age from newborn to two years old. The Roman Catholic Church reveres them as martyrs, so that if the festival of the Holy Innocents (28th December) falls on a Sunday, they are accorded the full privilege of a martyrs' day of red vestments and recital of the Gloria in Excelsis. They died so that the revelation of Christ could be revealed to humankind.

9

Birth control and self control

Sex and sexual problems within marriage

In the modern world, there have been far-reaching changes to the way in which people think about sex in relation to marriage. Contraception has enabled women to control their fertility, thus creating a new set of moral issues. Yet has this new freedom brought happiness?

It is hard for people to accept that the introduction of artificial contraceptives, which was heralded with such enthusiasm, has led to an increase in promiscuity and a reluctance to make marriages work if the sex life does not prove satisfactory or other fundamental things go wrong. Early-Christian thinking on women has not been much help to the female sex, as it has been overshadowed by Eve's responsibility for the Fall from the Garden of Eden. St Paul's writings on the subject of women frequently provoke anger. For example, he wrote the following about worship in the early Christian church at Ephesus: 'A woman ought to be quiet, because Adam was formed first and Eve afterwards, and it was not Adam who was led astray but the woman who was led astray and fell into sin.' (1 Timothy 2: 13,14)

In subsequent centuries difficulties and frequent loss of life in childbirth have made women grasp eagerly at the alternative offered by contraceptives. Women have inherited a harsh resentment against the fate which subjected them to a long subordination to men, and are suffering from the psychological effects of centuries during which men were the heads of household and women had no rights.

For hundreds of years, it was axiomatic that procreation was the main purpose and justification of intercourse. Infant mortality rates, even in the late nineteenth century, make appalling reading. Today, medical and nutritional advances have changed the whole demographic situation. Yet there is a tendency to play down the demographic effect of these reforms. The sticking point is always the fact that men and women are using the advances made in medicine and in society to assert their free will without reference to God.

There is extensive media coverage of the perceived threat of a population explosion which could threaten man's future. A constant challenge is presented by reports of millions of children who are born only to die of starvation and disease. Increasingly, sex is seen as a social recreation which must be controlled but which can assuage people's physical needs. Can the conception of children fit into this outlook, or is it becoming irrelevant?

The western world is confronted by a spiralling divorce rate, and yet people try to avoid responsibility for the far-reaching social effects of a broken marriage. Most are content to hand responsibility for the situation to the government. Yet the government should not be solely answerable. People will not accept that the foundering of so many marriages results directly from a breakdown in social and moral order.

The governments of Britain and other countries in the world have consistently supported the feminist movement and have tried to build a new society around the mother/child unit, fully aware of the social experiment that this has involved. Yet to survive, society has to be built on marriage. This can be proved historically, and yet statesmen and sociologists insist on promoting 'diverse family forms', 'single mothers and babies', 'multi-units' and an endless list of alternative social units. There is a wilful refusal to acknowledge publicly that a family is only complete when a mother, father and their children all live under one roof. This is still the ideal of most children. One teacher who discussed family life with her pupils found that children whose parents were divorced or separated felt their personal lives had been devastated. I remember a six-year-old boy who told me with an adult's anguish that he was determined to reunite his separated parents. His white, set face will always be with me, and the pain is all the greater because he did not succeed.

Unfortunately, the current liberal attitude to 'partnerships' is now so prevalent that women are automatically free to pursue a career, have children and a man of their choice to live with when they choose. The male position in the household has been downgraded to such an extent that young men wonder if they will ever be able to fulfil their traditional role of being the father and guardian of the home, leaving the woman free to exert her motherhood within the family unit.

There is no ready answer for such young men, as men and women pander to their sexual desires knowing they have the help of artificial contraceptives to prevent an unplanned pregnancy. The mere idea of stepping back into the inherited mould of a firm moral and legal structure which marriage provides is viewed with disgust and certainly ridicule by many people. The breakdown of belief in marriage has had more repercussions than the simple refusal of couples to marry. It extends to the denial of the entire series of exchanges involved in a marriage, when two groups of people witness the signing of a legally binding marriage contract. Additionally, there is a denial of the continuous family cycle, and the web of kinship and friendship which makes up the strongest threads in a community.

Instead, feminism has facilitated the creation of a new life style which insists on a two-wage income in a relationship and a demand for equality. The resultant pressure on women has left many hostile and a significant number ill. Men have become ill at ease as they witness the comprehensive denial of motherhood, which is valued less and less year by year. As time goes by, exhausted partners are often unable to fulfil the sexual aspect of their relationship and so instead decide to go their separate ways.

Today, emotions have overridden true compassion, and people show a black humour as they try to shrug off any responsibility towards family and friends. True compassion, if it is to exist within all relationships, cannot be a fleeting emotion, but a steadfast purpose to see a particular person or persons helped, however small their needs. As a society, our emotions have become superficial, and this is a major flaw in today's society which likes to appear politically correct and therefore compassionate to the outward eye. It has become so easy to avoid the difficult moments that occur in any relationships at home or away through this attitude. Yet behind the word 'compassion' lies a pure love which is a potent motivating force.

Why must the anguish of divorce and broken relationships affect society so deeply? The denial of the holiness of the wombs of women, and a widespread desire to ignore and kill the unborn child, can lead to incredible trauma which can stay with a person for the rest of their lives. Abortion has become an unacknowledged cancer eating at the heart of society, enfeebling it against the other attacks which occur naturally in a life span. But who will accept this as true?

Contraception – the slippery slope

Both the Egyptians and Babylonians noted the aphrodisiacal and contraceptive powers of various substances. One device was the sea-sponge soaked in lemon juice. Since ancient times, in every country and in every century, there has been a systematic study of means to prevent pregnancy. There has been no significant success until this century.

The well-established use of contraceptive devices should by now have effected an obvious transformation in society. It has become part of the feminist creed that only wanted children should be conceived. This has not in fact been the result of the use of artificial contraceptives: instead, women have taken advantage of these new controls over conception and have used them outside marriage. The free and widespread use of hormone-based contraceptives has contributed to an increase in the infertility rate and has made many women reluctant to have further children having once experienced the trauma of abortion. Yet modern science and research now allows women who want children to conceive in middle age, even if it means using other people's eggs or sperm, or even resorting to surrogate motherhood. At the heart of this tendency is the abandonment of an inherent belief in motherhood which suddenly reasserts itself just before the menopause with startling results.

Early this century, when contraceptive measures were being introduced to help curb Britain's rising population, there was vigorous opposition from all Christian churches. Later, informed discussion gave way to a system of family planning using artificial contraceptives within marriage, and a period of calm ensued. Unfortunately, the policies of Christian churches and government then diverged. Government ministers urged the supply of contraceptives to the unmarried, whether adult or teenagers. Many would insist that birth control is sometimes necessary for the unmarried, but surely nobody planned the scale of illegitimacy and abortion which has followed this measure? Throughout society, there is an increasing display of irresponsible sexual behaviour, divorce, sexually-transmitted diseases and cervical cancer.

Why has this deterioration occurred? There is a general assumption that contraceptives are necessary for effective birth control. Many mothers are happier to see their teenage daughters using contraceptives than to cope with the results of an unplanned pregnancy. They assume that they are doing their duty by their daughters, for recreational sex appears to have become a part of daily life. If a child is conceived, there is always the comfort of abortion 'on social grounds'. It is rare now to hear anyone suggest that mothers are responsible for promoting the virtues of chastity. These developments result from the reduced discipline imposed on teenagers, alongside the fact that all children are adults in the eyes of the state from the age of 18. The liberal media and the countless broken homes which surround every teenager compound the problem.

Contraception used without any reference to a moral framework leads to a slippery slope where respect for the foetus, or potential child, in the womb disappears. Contraceptives now fill the role of an aphrodisiac and appear to make people more caring and less prejudiced about the sexual act. That appearance is deceptive. Indeed, one widespread response to the availability of artificial contraceptives has been to encourage men and women to embark on an unhealthy pursuit of deviant sexual behaviour and to pursue the humanistic doctrine of self-interest.

In contrast, Christ's second great commandment was to love one's neighbour as oneself. Our Lord shows clearly that the child in the womb – whether wanted or unwanted – is our neighbour. In society today, the refusal to recognise the humanity of a child from conception is at the heart of so much modern-day disturbance. Sexual immorality and lack of respect for the unborn child are symptoms of a sick society which has moved away from Christian principles. In their hearts, people still want ideals, but they find it impossible to run two courses simultaneously, even though it is now recognised that artificial and natural methods are equally effective.

Contraceptives come in many forms:

1. Douches after intercourse.
2. *Coitus interruptus,* or the 'safe period'.
3. Chemicals in the form of foaming tablets, capsules, pessaries, jelly or aerosol foam.
4. A rubber sheath by a man or an occlusive diaphragm by a woman (the female condom).
5. Permanent intra-uterine devices that are removed after three years or before, if necessary.
6. Oral hormonal treatment which suppresses ovulation.

Young pregnant girls are often quoted as saying that they were never attracted by the clinical planning of contraceptive aids. Instead, they opted to take the risk of conceiving a child. Their approach is understandable. In a casual society, sexual activity tends not to be planned, but rather is drifted into as a result of too much drink, high emotion, or a response to unloving homes. Such an approach to sex does not correspond to the use of chemical contraceptives. Frequent reports in the national media show the results all too clearly.

Many people advocate use of the sheath, worn by the male partner, and the most widely used form of contraceptive after the Pill. The female condom depends on being in the right place at the right time.

Many women decide against using the intra-uterine device because they do not want a foreign body to be introduced into the uterus. The plastic loop, spiral and coil do not irritate the womb: inert and springy, they are easily replaced. Such methods of birth control are semi-permanent and are fitted by a doctor. They can increase menstrual bleeding, and the fitting may cause cramps and occasionally pelvic inflammation. Modern intra-uterine devices are impregnated with progesterone which reduces bleeding and may be used to off-set the effects of heavy periods.

Douching has been used for many years. It is performed immediately after intercourse as a natural means of avoiding conception. Doctors do not encourage its use, because it is not effective. Even so, it is almost certainly widely used.

Finally, the much-publicised Pill is seen as an easy way of practising birth control. However, regular media warnings about its effects on health have undermined confidence in it. The advantages are very real. The Pill comes with clear instructions and is easy to take. However, women users tend to be sensitive to the hormones, resulting in frequent headaches, sickness, nervousness, restlessness and a general feeling of being run-down. On top of this, the Pill can contribute to blood clots and high blood pressure or jaundice, although now it is recognised that the low-dosage Pill carries a low risk and prevents ovarian cancer. In general, the greater the dose of oestrogen, the greater the risk.

Sterilisation is also common, though some find it an unaccept-able approach to fertility control. *Coitus interruptus*, where the male withdraws before ejaculation, has generally fallen out of favour as a means of contraception as artificial methods which allow a more complete form of intercourse have become more widespread.

Why do women run all these risks? So that they can have sexual intercourse – an activity which is now regarded as an essential part of life?

In response to the health risks associated with artificial contraceptives, many people are turning to the Billings or mucus and temperature monitoring method, which is promoted in many parts of the world as a natural family-planning method. Most find it an enormous relief to know that family planning can be achieved by monitoring the woman's daily flow of mucus. When Dr John Billings started exploring the different types of mucus throughout the menstrual cycle, hundreds of women came forward to help him in his research. By the mid-1960s, after prolonged study, a set of guidelines was established for fertility control.

The Billings method has much to recommend it. Both husband and wife explore together the natural signs of fertility and infertility and practise this form of birth control in partnership. This eases the tensions which can so easily arise when one partner acts alone. Instead, the relationship is strengthened by the mutual trust involved and family life thus becomes more stable and secure. In this method, the physical sexual relationship has to be controlled, just like any other part of our anatomy. Yet, when controlled in the right way, it is a powerful communicator of love. However, couples often overlook the fact that using an ovulation thermometer can increase the effectiveness of this contraceptive method.

The way forward

A failure of the twentieth century is that people have not managed sexual activity and fertility in a civilised fashion. Instead, men and women have been encouraged to pursue any course which will make them feel young, attractive and sexually desirable. Women are paying a high price for their inability to understand what is happening to them when they use a steroid as a contraceptive, thus upsetting the balance of their bodies. All the warning signs have been deliberately played down by the media and government representatives as world population experts predict terrible disasters in the years ahead if the birth rate does not slow down. Meanwhile, the manufacturers of contraceptives have become business tycoons, who have capitalised on demand without stopping to consider the long-term effects of this medication on young women's developing bodies. Properly used, the combined Pill is judged to be safe and effective for most women non-smokers aged under 35. Sexual education should be promoted more, particularly within families rather than in schools and colleges. Mothers still have a part to play here.

Could unmarried teenagers be banned from using artificial contraceptives? Surely young men and women should once again be accommodated in separate hostels while attending college, with wardens who have a moral responsibility to protect their charges. Unfortunately, mothers are not prepared to protest against contraceptive aids for fear of seeming foolish. Yet many believe, deep down, that contraceptive aids are at least in part responsible for headaches, depression, infertility, miscarriages and even divorces that have occurred in their families.

Young teenagers have a right to be informed about the full consequences of sexual activity. Young girls in particular have the right to reject the tyranny of the Pill and its abuse by men who constantly seek sexual gratification and who assume that all women are carrying some form of birth control, either internally or in their handbags. Men ought not to be able to walk away if conception occurs, in the assured knowledge that abortion is available and advocated by medical practitioners when a pregnancy is unplanned.

The major ethical dilemmas continue to surround the point at which life begins. The argument about the 'slippery slope' deserves a hearing. No one advocates a nihilistic outlook, yet the desire for self-interest and the pursuit of pleasure is leading that way as more and more unborn children are killed in the womb. Those who try to point out the dangers have to be prepared for hostility, anger and verbal abuse. In the end, however, the stark horror aroused by confronting the hard realities will lead people to change their life styles and seek suitable support accordingly.

The British parliament determines the country's laws, and has established endless boards and commissions to deal with the many questions raised by day-to-day life. Concerned people need to spend time and energy appealing to these representatives. In the end, these efforts will result in a more compassionate society where doctors can once again function as kind, truthful and discreet friends of the family. The doctor's first task is to live up to a code of ethics which would protect life in the womb. In

79

renewed study of the Hippocratic Oath, the doctor will find relief for his or her conscience and will once again be able to treat patients as friends. I am sure that with more authoritative support, doctors would be happy to recommend continence outside marriage and natural family planning within marriage for those who can accept the self-restraint involved. But until that time arrives, the Pill will continue to pose problems, and its users may yet lobby for comprehensive controlled trials to ascertain its effects on health.

10

The message of motherhood for all women

The inheritance of sexual order for men and women

Religion in relation to sexual ethics has become almost totally irrelevant to the present age. Yet in medieval times the situation was entirely different. A whole culture and life style revolved around a common Christian faith. Medieval times were certainly brutish and cruel, yet the Christian Church managed to embody rationality and a common purpose. The Church presided over all matters relating to life and death, and her bishops and clergy made it their business to be involved in all aspects of living relating to the people whom they sought to turn to Christ.

The early Church's central role led her leaders to develop forms and ceremonies which could deal with habitual crises, such as birth, death and bereavement, which could give a rational meaning to many aspects of life.

People have not always tried to live by inherited instincts based on biological need, but instead have sought to bring all aspects of sexual activity into focus by reflecting on them so that they can be brought under a rational control. Yet medieval writers, such as Chaucer, describe a promiscuity which co-existed with Church life despite official condemnation by the Church authorities. The idea of exerting self-control is unthinkable to many present-day women. Motherhood is increasingly seen as a burden. Women prefer not to consider whether there might be a holiness involved in the conception of a child. Feminism has taught them the philosophy of the 'Me' syndrome.

But the inherited knowledge cannot be avoided, however much people try.

When Mary visited her cousin Elizabeth before the birth of Jesus, Elizabeth was an old woman who had become pregnant through divine grace. Her child would prepare the way for the coming of Christ. Yet, facing her young cousin Mary who was still in the early stages of her pregnancy, she called Mary 'the Mother of my Lord', so recalling all people to the uniqueness of Christ's conception, which would represent the union of the human with the divine. Despite Mary's undoubtedly painful circumstances, there is no doubt that she had been charged by God with an exceptional role in our eternal salvation, and that her role as a virgin and mother is instrumental for all of humanity.

Discussion about the role of Mary is often embarrassed. She does not fit into our strongly materialistic world. Christian thought holds up the sublime dignity of Mary, for she shares in the care shown by the Son for humanity, and as the mother of the Trinitarian God has the right to exert an authority over the minds and wills of men and women. Christians appeal to her motherhood because her motherly prayers and love can set them on fire with the love of God. It is impossible for Christians to avoid facing up to the submission of Mary to the will of God and her total trust in His Word.

At the core of Mary's role lies her example of obedience and faith. This is what young women, who have been brought up in a liberal society, find so difficult to accept. The idea that there may be an inner sanctuary within them which, when a child is conceived, reflects the conception of Christ in Mary, is of little relevance to them. Instead, women divide a sexual relationship with a man into two separate areas, one of sexual pleasure and the other of a deliberate act to conceive a child. This outlook is so prevalent, both in and outside marriage, that few are prepared to talk out boldly about the precious gift of life which can conceive and develop a child in the womb, and then give birth to a passionate love with motherhood which can astonish the observer.

Many people try to resist the purity of Mary, the mother of Jesus Christ, because they know that by following her example of obedience and motherhood, there is a risk of alienation from current trends. Nevertheless, most like to believe that they support certain moral principles and standards which harmonise with their Christian inheritance. But what have they been taught about that inheritance?

The clergy of the Christian churches can often appear unwilling to teach their faith to others, and instead seem to be wrestling openly with the moral problems posed by a fallen world. Authoritative traditional teaching is challenged at every stage, because every individual wants to put forward his or her own opinion. It seems that numerous Christians do not look on the Word of God as a living Word, where they can encounter the Holy Spirit. People seek to put their own interpretation on the Bible and are often not prepared to wait in prayer (sometimes for weeks or months) for the Holy Spirit to speak to them. Instead, the Holy Spirit is now seen by many as a focus of high emotion rather than prayerful meditation.

Traditionalist Christians know that if they meet with God daily through reading the Bible, they will be able to withstand opposition without and within. Regrettably, the power of sin and humankind's tendency to put God and self before the needs of others are totally underestimated. Love is an insipid emotion when it is only applied to self.

Nowhere is this more apparent than in the role of women in the Christian churches. The concept of women in religious life as the 'brides of Christ' is now often ridiculed, yet the words of a nun about her calling still ring true: 'I am so glad God called me so clearly, because it meant I could keep myself pure for Him.' In some religious orders of the Church of England, women who have served as 'brides of Christ', some of them for up to 50 years, are leaving their convents.

Many still like to believe that the battle of the sexes will be carried beyond the grave. This is a sad approach, for in God's kingdom, we are told in the Bible, there will be neither male nor female, for all will be lost in the wonder and praise of God. As a member of a contemplative movement, I have seen that in prayer, neither male nor female, young nor old, can dominate. Perhaps this is a pale reflection of what heaven will be like.

There is considerable room for improvement in the ways in which adolescents (including future mothers) are taught about sexual matters. Currently, there is a complete denial of any Christian values, under which chastity is not just a physical state of abstinence, but also a means of forging all kinds of personal relationships. Unfortunately, when people talk of chastity, they concentrate so hard on the factor of abstinence that most now think that this Christian calling in particular is inhuman, cold-blooded and most of all repressive of one's deepest emotions. The fact that Christ in his earthly life prized chastity above marriage and sexual activity is quietly swept under the carpet.

There is now a tendency to ally human sexual activity alongside that of the animal kingdom, so education authorities can show films to vulnerable young people of the reproductive processes in fish, animals and finally human beings. But what place does love, God's love in creation, have in this teaching? Surely this should form a central part of any sex education process to help young people cope with their clamouring impulses.

It seems that the teaching which approves of couples living and sleeping together at will is inspired by the belief that this way of life allows a natural release of tension which we, like animals, are unable to resist. It is hard to find a modern Christian philosophical text which will show a child that he or she should glorify God through self-control in the run-up to sexual maturity. In this outlook, the sexual aspect to relationships falls into place. Instead, however, society tends to look actively for a sexual aspect to any relationship, even when a perfectly innocent friendship has been formed between two people of the opposite or the same sex. The very word 'sex' now stands in isolation, and is associated only with the plain physical reality of the creative forces within each human being. Sex is seen as a clinical functional physical force outside spiritual control.

Regrettably, the world is haunted by a preoccupation with sex. Young and old, rich and poor, all are now alarmed at the moral disintegration which has been the result. Some blame modern social and economic pressures for the collapse. Others see it as

84

the result of a de-humanisation process which is the outcome of a highly technological society dominated by materialism. Few, however, are prepared to consider the spiritual insecurity which pervades society, and which leads so many to become entangled in unhappy relationships as they seek some kind of emotional anchorage.

Despite the constant discussion about sexual ethics, there is a reluctance to speak out boldly about the motherhood which forms a natural part of creation and an integral piece of Judeo-Christian culture. There is a refusal at every level to teach that motherhood is intertwined with inherited biological impulses and is the driving force in a woman's psyche. The physical care of a child is considered without any coherent analysis of the unseen forces which develop with a baby's birth. These forces exist in every woman to be developed either through giving birth or by developing a creative process in their professional lives.

If these forces are starved or denied, they weaken or fade away altogether in a killing-off of one's motherhood. Many women try to run away or dodge these forces by saying they don't exist, and drive them away to their own detriment. In the long run, this denial will result in deep, disturbing emotions over which women will have little or no control.

The motherhood which is to be found in all women

As a woman brought up in a generation where many women were unmarried following the First World War, I followed my peers in knowing such women as 'war widows', even though they had never married and had no children. Because so many men had died in the war, they had no opportunity to marry, so they fulfilled themselves elsewhere. This they did, using their latent motherhood in many exciting ways, particularly teaching. They have left behind them many wonderful schools and generations of children to whom they taught the Christian faith.

These women were never laughed at because of their single status. In fact, their purity was much respected, and the communities around them encouraged them to express their maternal

85

instincts. They worked in the community fearlessly, knowing that the people around them understood their predicament.

Today, the scenario is very different. There is no such quiet confidence among the unmarried. By unmarried I mean women who have either decided not to marry, who have had no opportunity of marriage or have not sought out a partner. Such women keep a low profile, knowing all too well that they may be laughed at or have jeering comments made about their sexuality.

It is almost unnerving to meet such singularly pure people. They have become a rarity in society, and their way of life is provocative and challenging. Many of their friends do not hesitate to tell them to go out and 'get a man', so that they can lose their innocence and become the same as everybody else.

Even in the late nineteenth century, falling standards were evident. Unfortunately, the decline has continued, and many turn and blame each other. Headteachers in previous generations were aware of what was happening, and would say openly that mothers were not teaching their children any Christian belief. As a result, church attendance was in decline, and knowledge of the Bible was less widespread. Headteachers would not dare to make such comments today. Even so, parents still have a lingering assumption that the large body of unmarried women who did so much to teach the faith following the First World War, is still there. They are shocked when they learn that the duty now lies with them at home.

Parents who do not want to teach their children the Christian faith themselves now look around carefully for a school that will do it for them alongside normal primary school education. They may even take their children along to Sunday school at the local church. Once the object has been achieved, they abandon all pretence of a Christian order in their own home. Young mothers sheepish about their own inadequate practice of Christian faith and outlook in their own personal lives, try to place the responsibility for religious order with others, in the belief that someone else will always be there to do the job for them. Most, however, know in their own hearts that such teaching is most effective when it comes with a mother's love.

People try to justify this type of outlook by speaking out

against women who do not seek any sexual relationship or who do not conceive a child outside marriage. Their clarity of vision is disconcerting to those who have chosen a different way of life. Most people understand, however, that today's fluid society will not cement into a recognisable whole, and that the population is living without a moral focus. Morally, the world has moved into such uncharted seas that it is impossible to predict where its chosen route will lead.

It is easy for Christians to forget that, unlike any club or college, the Church's moral framework is not just for its members. Rather, it is a declaration of God's love and will for all men and women at all times and stages of their development. Faced with crises of conscience, most people tend to say that they live in a post-modernist culture where Church values have no status. Even so, they are hesitant to offer opinions on the issue of motherhood, because they know instinctively that it is a force which plumbs the depths of a woman's psyche.

Even more embarrassing for Christians is the fact that Christianity's goal is not only to explain its beliefs to the world, but to change it and transform it by faith and example. Christianity can help hard-pressed men and women to live with integrity and fulfilment and, in short, to find salvation. First of all, though, the challenging ethics of purity and chastity which are advocated by the Christian Church need to be confronted and absorbed. Their authority will not go away.

Is purity appropriate or achievable today?

A country's legal framework can educate public opinion, and it is surely time for the legal profession to make a fresh study of the 1957 Wolfenden Report which released schools from any obligation to teach theology, sociology or psychology. The report had a devastating effect on Britain's Christian inheritance and culture, and, nearly 40 years after the adoption of its recommendations, an investigation into its moral principles and assumptions and their consequences is long overdue.

So much is written about sex that sometimes people forget the effect the act has on the male and female genders. A male orgasm is a single act which brings instant relief. While a woman may have one or several orgasms, the act of sex opens up the possibility of initiating a whole cycle of events ending in gestation, birth and motherhood.

Young people, although physically mature, are still mentally and emotionally unstable, and are usually unable to control the highly-charged emotions aroused by sex. They are in urgent need of support and guidance, but what they are offered by the adult world is of little help and certainly lays down no guidelines for them to follow. Nowhere is the cynical irresponsibility of today's affluent society more obvious than in its failure to honour chastity and to guide teenagers into a moral way of life.

Sometimes, events move in a full circle, and this is what appears to be happening today. More and more young people are slowly finding their way towards an alternative attitude towards pre-marital sex. Their parents may believe that sexual liberation is unstoppable, but they do not always take into account the fact that each generation looks forward with hope and sets itself ambitious goals. Parents and teenagers know only too well that once sexual contact has been made, it is unlikely to stand as a single act, but is likely instead to lead to a series of sexual encounters.

Christians, particularly parents, must take a closer look at the questions raised by chastity in today's society. Parents hesitate to confront their children, and it is often all they can do to prevent their daughters becoming sexually active until they are 16 and able to go on the Pill. Yet a young girl who is faced with an unplanned pregnancy will frequently find herself thrown out of her home if she wants to keep the child. All too often, her parents do not want the responsibility of bringing up another generation.

There are wonderful examples of grandmothers who have taken charge of their unplanned grandchild and encouraged their child (for that is what she is) to go back to school or to work. These unacknowledged grandmothers are ready to take responsibility for what is frequently their own failure to give sufficient care to their teenage daughters. They may well have some salient

88

The Archangel Michael
the protector of life.

The hard climb to
Heaven.

Eve and the Serpent.

Our Lady of Fatima. The Icon of family life.

The Announcement.

Christian approaches
the Heavenly City.

The Indian Madonna
and the gift of life.

The breaking of
Motherhood.
The symbol of the home.

thoughts which could contribute towards the debate about the meaning of chastity. In the Christian context, chastity ought to mean a joyful coming together of sexual love in the framework of marriage which constitutes a complete and exclusive mutual self-giving between two persons. But what examples can they follow?

Only those who have led an upright life themselves until marriage or as single people can publicly offer a way ahead for young people. I am sure many people secretly congratulated the recently-retired Archbishop of York when he stated publicly that he was celibate until he married. How many would admit to the same to their families and friends? The answer is, not many. Most young people now believe that the first passport into adulthood is sexual experience.

11

*The damaging effects of sexual
hormonal development*

Pope John Paul II said in a sermon in 1978: 'Respect for truth can be a costly virtue, but it is armed with that virtue that Poland has come through her first millennium, and only armed with that virtue can the nation enter the second millennium.' These words may equally be applied to the western world. As we enter the next millennium, can we say that we too respect truth? And in particular, do we have any respect for the truth about the effects of hormones on a developing child in the womb?

Although this century has seen an explosion of interest in health and healing, more effort is expended in finding cures rather than preventive treatment. The Bible is quite clear that at the root of all that tarnishes the world, including disease, lies humanity's sinning against the authoritative Word of God. The coming of Jesus Christ allowed His death as He gave His life for us on the cross. The shedding of Christ's blood heralded a new era of forgiveness and fellowship between God and humanity. This trust is being betrayed by today's society as people try to hide the effects of contraception on the unborn child.

In 1978, 16,000 women in Jerusalem took part in a large-scale study of the Pill, carried out by the National Institute of Child Health and Development in Bethesda, USA. The study established that if women became pregnant as soon as they came off the Pill, their children were more likely to be born with vascular skin abnormalities. Along with underweight females or women aged over 35, these women were more likely to have a miscarriage or an abnormal child. It was also shown that women

90

who had been on the Pill ran a higher risk of miscarriage, stillbirth, twins and babies with cardiovascular abnormalities (*Sexual Chemistry,* by Dr Ellen Grant, p.252).

Before the twentieth century, medical ethics in the western world were virtually identical to Christian ethics. Today, many doctors are quite prepared to share their lack of faith with their patients in a nonchalant way, in the belief that all shades of opinion are equally valid if conscientiously held. The British Medical Association's *Handbook of Medical Ethics* gives the following advice concerning abortion, which may also be applied to pre-natal abnormalities resulting from hormone-based contra ceptives: 'If a doctor is uncertain, he should always consult other colleagues, follow his conscience, and act in the best interest of his patient.' [not patients] But how can the conscience be a moral guide if doctors' consciences are divided?

If questioned, a doctor would probably admit that he could only judge a given situation in a personal capacity, and would aim to resolve it to the best of his ability. He would not be interested in what pre-dated his patient's visit, although after dealing with the immediate situation, he might be willing to give guarded advice to the patient for the years ahead. For example, if a child is born with irreversible brain damage but is not likely to die in the near future, that child can suddenly become a sociopolitical problem as the search begins for valuable hospital beds and scarce resources. A utilitarian philosophy can be applied, but the idea that any possible deficiency in pre-natal care may have contributed to the condition might be avoided. Up to now, the courts have erred on the side of the parents, finding hospitals guilty of negligence in order to provide the parents with funds for the care of the child. It is possible for so-called birth injuries to pre-date delivery. Hopefully, the National Health Scheme Trusts recently introduced in the United Kingdom will help to reverse this approach.

So, although health care promotes the common good, it can promote the wrong decision. There is probably no sphere in which a counter-balance is more needed than in medical ethics. The conscience of the utilitarian and practically-minded doctor will accept any ethical dilemma as a personal challenge, as opposed to a Christian doctor who tries to obey God in all areas.

Hormones and the cycle of life

Many anxious women living in North London can reveal their belief that one of the greatest hazards in the water supply is the effects of the contraceptive hormones given to them which enters the water system. This is because sewage waste is treated and then re-circulated as tap water. For the past ten years, deformed hermaphrodite trout have been found near water outlets. Ethinyloestradiol and mestranol, which are given to millions of women on the Pill or receiving hormone replacement therapy, are particularly prevalent and now constitute one part per billion in the reproductive systems of animals and fish (*Sexual Chemistry*, by Dr. Ellen Grant). How should we approach this kind of data?

It is useful to picture a set of scales, where extra weight on either side will swing the balance. A girl with an unplanned pregnancy knows she has the legal right to destroy her child and that civil law is on her side, yet she is aware of the phrases 'respect for human life' and 'protecting the innocent', and knows she is contemplating the taking of a potentially healthy human life.

To a Christian, respect for human life forms part of God's plan, and boundaries have been set over the centuries to help him or her to live according to this ideal. Those boundaries are no longer secure as God's law is seen to stand in the way of people's desires. There is now little or no compassion for the child developing in a woman's womb, because it conflicts with feminist ideals. People who believe in the sanctity and cycle of human life often find themselves attacked as a result by aggressive idealists. Those who understand that God gave all human beings a custodianship of all life need to study St Paul's words: 'God created all fullness to be found in him and through him to reconcile all things to him, everything in heaven and everything on earth, by making peace through his death on the cross.' (Colossians 1: 19-20)

92

Responsibility

Man's estimate of the worth of a human life tends to be based on social usefulness, and it is not unusual to hear someone say that so-and-so has a good quality of life in spite of age or other problems. Yet such is the fear of responsibility surrounding the prospect of a physically or handicapped child that medical authorities can bring all sorts of pressures to bear on the unfortunate mother-to-be. Murderers arouse a collective noble anger in the population, but the killing of a child in the womb prompts hospital administrators simply to cover their tracks. In fact, people's consciences have been blunted and their will vacillates when it comes to public decisions.

Yet hospital administrators deserve our compassion, for after all they are administering a gigantic organisation which has had to adjust to endless political, social and minority interference. They have to cope with reports about the number of terminations which are performed in day-care centres. This situation is a discredit to a country which avowedly bases itself on Christian laws, but instead appears to have let secular humanists and the market economy define its values.

Humankind is of infinite worth to God, even in the womb. John the Baptist rejoiced in the womb of his mother Elizabeth when Mary came to visit after Christ's conception. Men and women are not superior animals who can be put down at will. They know that Christ loves them, but they cannot escape responsibility for God's assessment of a human being's worth, even in the womb. The womb is a holy place, designed and organised by a loving Father so that it can do extraordinary things to create children in His image.

Society needs an ideal of Christian life which is not devoted to an inward-looking ideology or allegiance or even a political party which denies the unique identity of the child in the womb. Jesus came in human form to show his love for us, and he gave his life for us. Now people are being tempted away from their obligation and obedience to God.

St Peter wrote to Christians in Asia Minor to encourage them in times of trial and persecution, and told them that their true worth was shown by sharing in Christ's sufferings. 'Free your minds, then, of encumbrances; control them, and put your trust in nothing but the grace that will be given you when Jesus Christ is revealed. Do not behave in the way that you liked to before you learnt the truth; make a habit of obedience.' (1 Peter 1:13,14)

12

The zygote, the priest, and the call of God

Humanity and the zygote

When people talk about how the complexities of bio-ethics relate to the coming of Jesus Christ, they can suddenly pause and say with some wonder: 'Our Lord must have been a zygote at some stage of his development!' In fact, deeper thought is required. The zygote is produced by the fusion of the male and female gametes or spermatozoon and ovum respectively, so forming a fertilised ovum. When we talk about our Lord being a zygote, we are in fact referring to a mystery of conception which goes beyond human understanding. His mother, Mary, was a virgin when the conception took place. Christ was fully human and fully divine, and yet all humans started off as a zygote.

So let's try to understand a little of this process, even if it is only to establish how conception occurs. The ovum, or egg, is produced in the ovary and is then fertilised in the Fallopian tube. The zygote develops only when a sperm succeeds in fertilising the egg. Millions of sperm are ejaculated by the male in the vagina in each act of intercourse. The meeting of a sperm with the egg causes the *corpus luteum* to continue to produce progesterone so that the lining of the uterus is maintained to await implantation.

After this implantation, the zygote, now known as an embryo, is a hollow ball of cells or blastocyst which produces the placenta. This gradually takes over the hormone production from the *corpus luteum*.

95

Why must these processes be written about in such detail here? It is to show the intricacy of the process in so far as it is understood by man. All the above activity is influenced by the hypothalamus at the base of the brain acting through the pituitary gland. This hypothalamus hormone is automatically brought into operation, and is under the control of hormones and the nervous system. It is mainly concerned with 'vegetative' functions, such as the temperature of the body, body weight and appetite, sexual behaviour, blood pressure and fluid balance. It provides the physical basis for the emotions and ultimately for evolutionary genetics.

It would not be out of place here to write a separate book about genetics in relation to medicine and a discussion on the origin of species and who and what we are. But this book is concerned with love, God's love at work within creation. It is the most powerful force of all, because it is creative. This love is a deep, embedded love, which men and women cannot do without in the process of procreation. When a man and woman first see their own child, they experience an immediate physical, emotional and spiritual bonding. This is their own child, of their own blood. It is this overwhelming force that scientists are currently trying to control and guide along lines which have no ethical foundations, for sex now falls into two categories – recreational or reproductive.

Although this is an avowedly secular age, the hidden depths within each human being cannot be denied. But it is becoming increasingly difficult to be aware of them, as the creative process becomes entangled with the ever-widening horizons of human knowledge and achievement. Few give any thought to the danger of sinning against God's ordinance, even though humankind was told to submit to the creative order by a loving God, using knowledge as a tool to achieve this end. Endless church committees have advised extreme caution when debating such a 'hot' issue, but on the whole the outcome is uncertain rather than dogmatic. Few wish to challenge the 'rights' of women to have a child when they please.

The root of the problem lies in the separation of the sexual act and procreation. This has helped men and women to avoid mutual commitment in the case of an unplanned pregnancy. In the years ahead, however, the population level may fall sufficiently low for the prevailing government to legislate for such unplanned children to be born, so that they can join the work-force. At the moment, though, the economy is an entirely secular structure, and parliamentarians refuse to become involved in what they see as a moral maze. For them, Christian discipleship should be acknowledged but given no commitment.

Jesus Christ himself was at some stage an embryo. This very fact forces Christians to recognise the hand of God at work in every conception. Theological and legal concepts of when a foetus can be called a human being are moving earlier and earlier into pregnancy. Ultrasound scans can show a baby's heart-beat as early as three or four weeks after conception. Added to this, a woman's intuition can tell her when she is pregnant without any medical tests, and the 'glow of motherhood' can settle on her at a very early stage.

For all this, nothing, it seems, will prevent women from accepting the effects of synthetic steroid tablets on their repro-ductive systems, which so alter the endometrical environment that human 'seeds' cannot implant. In fact, the moral maze which surrounds us is concentrated around the woman's reproductive system – a consideration which few care to discuss openly. Yet there is more to women than their reproductive systems!

Reluctantly, one must accept that society has reached a stage where childbearing is regarded as a woman's right, and where scientific medicine is there to satisfy demand for a child. It is no longer acceptable for adopted children to fill the emptiness left by infertility, as they have in past centuries. A mountain of despair has resulted, not only of the women who weep for the child or children they aborted, but also of the prospective parents whose wish to adopt is thwarted because there are no children available.

The principal ethical dilemma faced by many gynaecologists is the extravagant waste of life. One fifth of all conceptions is deliberately aborted. Nobody is willing to admit that the killing of a child is a form of infanticide, and the liberal attitude to abor-tion is inevitably leading to a diminished respect for all human life. Today, all age-groups tend to view a visit to their general practitioner with apprehension. It is difficult for them to pinpoint the reason. Is it unreasonable to suggest that it stems from their sense that doctors have lost their belief that they are there to save life rather than destroy it?

'You created my inmost self, knit me together in my mother's womb,' says the psalmist. 'You knew me through and through, my being held no secrets from you . . . Your eyes could see my embryo. In your book all my days are inscribed.' (Psalm 139:13,15)

Humanity and the priest

Despite the growing tendency to view unborn human life as expendable, the trend contrasts strongly with the order placed on all humanity by a loving God. Yet abortion actually involves, in every single case, the conscious and deliberate killing of a living and developing human being. It does not matter whether this developing human being is called a child, an embryo or even a foetus. The essential point is that it is alive and human.

Unfortunately, details of reproduction and the facts of abortion, as discussed in this book, can offend people's finer feelings, and there can be a tendency to sweep this type of debate under the carpet. The fact that a certain 'priesthood' may be conferred on every woman at her conception is unacceptable to most people, and few will even discuss the idea. Yet over the Church's 2,000-year history, the most profoundly holy and intelligent theologians have thought otherwise.

Yet the idea of the institution of priesthood, alongside that of sacrifice, is found in almost all great religions. Sacrifice is central to the creation of new life and motherhood. Today, a struggle is under way, because the role of the Eucharist is under threat from new ideas about the role of males and females. Many may challenge the idea that sacrifice is central to motherhood, but the ultimate example is offered by Mary, the mother of Jesus Christ. She is the high priestess of the Christian Church by virtue of working with the divine.

98

When he lived on earth as a man, Jesus looked forward to the speedy end of the Jewish animal sacrifices. It was common practice for all religions, including that of the early Hebrews, to offer a living creature to God. Worshippers would share in a 'peace' offering, when worshippers would divide the flesh between them, or in the 'burnt' offering, when the flesh was destroyed. These sacrifices were performed regularly, alongside offerings of cereal, oil and wine. Jesus came with a new covenant with humankind so that the need for sacrifice could be swept away.

In early Church teaching, the Eucharistic offering was called a sacrifice by virtue of its immediate relation to the sacrifice of Christ. From this, Christians have commonly understood that an individual's conscious obedience, whether active or passive, to the will of God, is also a sacrifice which can be offered to God the Father in imitation of, and in union with, the sacrifice of Christ.

These days, there is a tendency to concentrate on St Peter's teaching on a universal priesthood: 'But you are a chosen race, a kingdom of priests, a holy nation, a people to be a personal possession to sing the praises of God who called you out of the darkness into his wonderful light.' (1 Peter 9) The idea of a priesthood in the Christian ministry was a gradual development and did not really apply until the end of the second century.

At first, there were strict rules concerning celebration of the Eucharist and whether a penitent could receive in the absence of a bishop. The Eucharist was usually celebrated by presbyters who belonged to a board of 'elders' – a system very similar to that found in Jewish synagogues. The presbyters' authority came from the bishops. In its developing form, Christian priests could administrate, teach and consecrate the Elements in a similar manner to Jewish priests. Later, as Christianity spread, priests were sent to outlying regions, so giving rise to the medieval doctrine of a priesthood with no benefice. This had become customary by the eleventh century. Eucharistic theology and the obligation of confession quickly developed, and the priest came to be regarded as the representative of God to the people rather than the reverse. The priest's supernatural powers were emphasised in the Middle Ages, and there was tendency to see the priest almost exclusively in relation to the Mass. After the Reformation there was a sharp divide, and the word 'clergyman' came to be used to avoid all the implications contained in 'priest'. In spite of this conflict of ideas, both men and women fitted into an established order, particularly in relation to the order of creation and the doctrine of the Eucharist. Yet all this was thrown into confusion in the Anglican communion when the idea of a female priesthood was raised as a viable proposition. Laws have been swept aside to maintain recent developments, and new ones have been formulated to promote and foster them in societies which have been curiously slow to adopt a similar outlook.

In the twentieth century, Christians are so confused about the Eucharistic sacrifice that even the word 'holy' is rarely attributed to it. Surely this is when we must go back to our conscience which bears witness to the moral standards we possess within us. All people are born with a conscience, and they experience its activity from early childhood – it is not for nothing that many people talk of 'an inner voice' while others talks of the revealed Word of God. The Bible describes the conscience as 'bearing witness', and Christians know that its effectiveness is increased by use and through grace. In fact, the conscience is a mediator between the law of God and the will of man. Surely our consciences must be active when we see evolutionary humanism developing a system of thought and belief which denies the uniqueness of the sexes in relation to the Eucharist.

Jesus summarised Christian doctrine as first of all the love of God, and secondly that love of one's neighbour as oneself. But if people deny the uniqueness of a conception (which calls forth a sacrificial motherhood) they are showing the sickness of today's society. If we truly love God, and see the Incarnation as our ultimate example and a sign for all women, we would aim for a re-acceptance of the principles from which we are retreating, rather than go along with a sick society.

The refusal to acknowledge the sacrificial role of motherhood can leave many people bewildered. Going so far as to link motherhood to the sacrificial role of priesthood can enrage them. The World Population Conference in Cairo attracted 20,000 delegates and their supporters, all of whom wanted to promote the idea that the sexual function can and should be separated from its biological purpose – procreation. It emerged that efforts to promote the use of condoms and hormone-based contraceptives had not succeeded in stabilising population growth. Yet to take sex away from its traditional, solemn, matrimonial context is to strip it of all mystery and wonder and place it on the same level as a trip to the cinema.

Is it ethical for medical practitioners to implement such a policy formulated by political idealists, without referral to patients who accept the word of their doctor to control their fertility without a moral framework? Is it ethical to totally abandon our Judeo-Christian inheritance on which our laws are based?

In Britain the state deems it politic and, at the very least, legitimate, to take the lives of 20 per cent of one section of the population – unborn children. These children form a minority, and a weak one at that, but the decision to take their lives poses a challenge to God, our creator. One of the state's primary functions is to protect minorities whenever they come under threat, yet this function is ignored in the case of unborn children. The Christian churches are uneasy and have lost their footing in the face of the state's uncompromising stance.

Do we now have to wait for society's distress to accumulate until people acknowledge God with shouts of 'My God, my God', for a change in law?

The call of God and creation

In the 1950s, the Family Planning Association – then run on a voluntary basis – was struggling to prevent married women from having too many children. Even then, the association pressed for legalised abortion for married women, but Christian standards prevailed. Not until the 1970s did unmarried women become the main clients of the then well-established family planning clinics. As a result, it became usual for women to have a series of sexual partners. Cervical cancer and the abortion rate increased, particularly among teenagers. Any young doctor trying to join a general practice was expected to prescribe the Pill and if he or she voiced objections on health grounds, they were not tolerated. Where does this leave our free will?

Years ago, before he became Pope, Cardinal Wojtyla stressed the principle of free will in a pastoral letter. 'St Stanislaw (1030-79) has become the patron saint of moral and social order in this country [Poland]. He dared to tell the King himself that he is bound to respect the law of God. The age-old veneration of St Stanislaw is, in fact, a confession of the truth that moral law is the foundation of social order.' St Stanislaw, the patron saint of Poland, became Bishop of Cracow in 1072 and in that capacity came into conflict with the reigning king who murdered him with his own hand when St Stanislaw was celebrating Mass. St Stanislaw was prepared to listen to the call of God, and face the consequences. Are today's Christians equally ready?

I felt a strange supernatural pressure at a time when all of my six children were still young enough to be fully dependent on me. I understood it to be a call from God, although I had never sought this type of experience, and it resulted in years of sleepless nights. Finally, however, I had to accept that the pressure I felt did not come from God. It reflected the eternal conflict of good and evil, a conflict which can confront anybody who lives on earth. I realised I could protect myself and my family best by avoiding the new avenues offered by this experience. The conflict was too great for me to confront as a wife and mother. I am now prepared to declare publicly that women owe it to themselves not to try and explore such avenues.

The world needs a greater readiness among its population to listen more closely to those who have abandoned the outside world in order to face and confront the forces of evil. If a woman is truly called by God, she must abandon all desires to be a wife and mother because celibacy is an integral part of the calling and commitment of men and women whom God has chosen. If she tries to answer the call without having decided against marriage and children, she denies a natural order and a pattern of behaviour which was adopted in the early Church and ordained by the apostles. It is unfortunate that so many established ideals have been dropped in recent years. It has left people transforming fantasies into ideals and has led to great suffering among women. The life of Mary, the Mother of God, reflects no such fantasies. Time and again, the New Testament records that Mary 'pondered' certain events in her heart. Until women follow her example, and reflect deeply on their role in God's plan, they face a future of distress and bewilderment.

Men and women are starved of love as the ugly side of feminism reveals itself. Natural courtship is now almost a thing of the past, and most women advise their friends: 'If you want a man, get him into bed first.' The time is ripe for change. Secular enthusiasms have lost their allure, and only the wilfully ignorant truly believe that society has reinvented itself in the run-up to the third millennium.

13

The historical tradition of natural law and order

The difficulties of modern society are perhaps most apparent in the legal approach to parenting. Parents may encounter doctors who defend teenagers' autonomy and who can count on the law to back them up. In the UK, this became particularly apparent when the Roman Catholic activist Victoria Gillick fought unsuccessfully for the right to be informed if her teenage daughters were prescribed the Pill. Society is besieged by theorists who try to influence people's views. Many have given in to these pressures, unwilling to appear politically incorrect to their friends and colleagues.

People want to live in a secure legal framework, but somehow an entirely different scenario is prompted by the prospect of abortion. Since the Abortion Act of 1967, society has developed an attitude of mind which allows abortion for social reasons without taking into account the long-term effects. Christians want the legal system to conform to Christian ideals and teaching, but the confusion in society as a whole is so great that it is now easier to accept abortion as a way of life than to try and prevent it.

Natural law and order in relation to abortion

Numerous moral and political opinions may be conscientiously held and put into practice in today's society, but such a broad spectrum of opinions are held over the taking of life from a woman's womb that it seems impossible to reach a rational conclusion. As a result, any abortions are hidden under a veil of secrecy. The current abortion laws are interpreted liberally in the absence of any Act of Parliament which aims to protect the child *in utero*. Can this be right? Should natural justice and law be more visible in this context? Surely any discussion of the issue should accord moral status to the human embryo, rather than designate it as a mere collection of cells.

Most lawyers would insist that the law is not a suitable instrument for the enforcement of morality in these circumstances. Yet society looks to the law for an opinion on this issue. The churches speak out against abortion, as they have from the beginning, but their resistance has been worn down over the years as the insidious infiltration of diverse outlooks have taken effect within their ranks. Looking at a pregnant woman, people try their best to see her as one person, not as someone who is going to give birth to a child who is the Christian's unseen neighbour in Christ. On the other hand, if she acknowledges cheerfully that she is expecting a child, people relax and are happy to rejoice with her. Only an assurance that the child is wanted can put an end to the embarrassed silence with which we condemn ourselves in the face of confrontational feminism. Feminism simply cannot afford to admit the personal identity of the unborn child, because that would erode what its supporters are trying to achieve: women's freedom to do whatever they like with their own bodies.

Natural order has long since been relegated to the background, as society seeks to achieve equality of the sexes as its greatest goal. But if society is to have any stability, there must be some sort of discrimination between the sexes for the sake of the family unit. Yet this fact is denied. It is surely time for society to set legal boundaries establishing whether and to what extent sexual discrimination would be permissible in order to give a proper value to life in the womb, rather than simply intoning the mantra of equal rights.

There is a strong belief in society that only women who are competent should be allowed to choose whether or not to proceed with a pregnancy. But how competent are teenage girls of making choices about the destiny of their unborn children? Is it right that they should be able to decide to terminate the pregnancy? Or should they face a legal requirement to proceed with the pregnancy and offer the child for adoption? Natural law seems to side with the latter view.

What is natural law?

Natural law establishes the family unit where a number of individuals are linked by a set of enduring relationships, the most important of which are those engendered by the birth process. Children are born into families and relationships which are permanent rather than transitory. Relationships extend across the generations and the birth of a child has implications for the parents and for the wider group of surrounding individuals.

The quality of relationships within the family is a particular concern of modern society. There is a tendency to deny that any conception within the family complex has implications for the whole family, even when the child is aborted. Instead, abortions are concealed from the rest of the family unit.

People are only now becoming aware that children conceived by artificial insemination by donor (AID) or in-vitro fertilisation (IVF) using an anonymous donor of sperm or eggs, are denied their perceived rights, duties, obligations and expectations by this same secrecy, which conceals and distorts family relationships. Yet emotions within the family can run high, and relatives may be horrified if the law denies them access to their blood relations. They know that relationships may be harmed both in permanence and in quality.

Until recently it was accepted that the father's role encompassed the provision of half the genetic material which would contribute to the genetic make-up of his child, and half the responsibility for the care and nurture of the child until it reached adulthood. The mother, on the other hand, has three separate roles. She provides the other half of the child's genetic make-up, is responsible to nurture the child from birth, and carries the child during the nine-month gestation period of pregnancy. This, too, forms part of a natural order.

Over the centuries, this natural order has been confirmed and reinforced by law. Today, however, this is no longer the case. Children may have more than one mother- or father-figure if their natural parents divorce, and the range of relationships within a family circle that has been extended through divorce can become so diverse that it is incomprehensible to the outsider. Clearly, not everybody marries or lives as part of a family, but most people look to the family unit for love, companionship and security even when that unit becomes more remote or diverse after divorce or marriage breakdown. When family life collapses, a compassionate community should do all in its power to protect and care for the casualties. The bitter sequels to family break downs are known to have far-reaching and catastrophic effects on estranged parents and their children. Most people have read newspaper reports or have heard accounts from acquaintances of non-payment of maintenance. Fierce legal battles rage over property and children. Even the tax legislation does not appear to take natural law into account when it apparently penalises marriage and gives little or no recognition to those mothers who stay at home to rear their families.

If we believe in natural law, we should be lobbying for an effective family policy that acknowledges the humanity of a child from conception. That child must have its life and integrity protected. Children deserve a world which can offer them all the best chances of development. Their good is the responsibility not only of their parents, but also of the wider community.

Most people want to protect their families, following their own inherited intuition. But, unsure of that intuition, they have instead opted to go along with society's utilitarian reasoning, hoping against hope that the central conflict between law and morality within the family may yet resolve itself. But most know that any individual needs both respect for their autonomy and the opportunity to live in a loving and caring community in order to flourish fully as a human being.

The historical tradition of abortion

The 4,000-year-old Jewish legal code is one of the most ancient in the world. It views any interference with the process of human reproduction, including abortion, with utter abhorrence. The assembly-line approach to human reproduction is unacceptable in the Jewish understanding. Yet Jewish law states firmly that a child does not reach full human status until birth. How did it reach this conclusion?

Jewish law relies on two Biblical sources: 'Anyone who by violence causes a death, must be put to death,' (Exodus 21:12) and 'If people, when brawling, hurt a pregnant woman and she suffers a miscarriage but no further harm is done, the person responsible will pay compensation as fixed by the woman's master, paying as much as the judges decide.' (Exodus 22:21) The interpretation given by Jewish law is that disposal of life within the womb is not a capital offence.

Nevertheless, the destruction of potential human life is seen as a grave offence by the Jewish community. Masturbation (which donors of semen need to do to produce a sample) is regarded as a serious infringement of moral law. Abortion is condemned except where the pregnancy puts the mother's life at risk. Abortion of the unborn handicapped child is tolerated, but objections grow according to how far the pregnancy has progressed. Nevertheless, the Jews hold firm to the belief that social or economic factors should not be sufficient grounds for termination of human life – in stark contrast to the large-scale social abortions performed in modern society.

The Jews also insist that a child has an unalienable right to a biologically identifiable mother and father. Through this insistence, they reinforce family life and maintain it through thick and thin.

But have Jewish attitudes spread to countries in the West which base their law on Jewish and Roman inheritance? England has a different approach. Its laws have been inherited in the main from the Anglo-Saxons, and were too entrenched to be overwhelmed by the Norman Conquest. So they continue to form the basis of common law, and have been modified for use in many parts of the globe which came under English influence, including the USA.

Behind all this legal activity lies a conflict between the inherited human genetic urge to express itself in the sexual act, and the love which is found in the family unit. These two forces form the foundation of human nature, because they are fundamental to evolution. Nevertheless, they have to be controlled by compassionate yet firm laws.

These forces have been so great that they have led to situations where there have been far too many children for countries to support. The urge to breed can be all-consuming. In the eighteenth century, about three-quarters of all children born in England were dead by the age of five. Death was part of everyday life. Yet there are still people who remember stillborn children who were put in a box lined with flowers for the sexton to bury in a churchyard. These memories, which are now almost lost to us, show that there always used to be respect for life in the womb. Even if it was stillborn, there was deeply held belief that the child must be buried in a churchyard.

It seems that modern society no longer has the vast stores of biological energy which were controlled through a natural wastage while conforming to natural law and the country's legal framework. Instead, the reproductive apparatus seems to be allocated equal status to a bulb in a pot and sexual activities are performed purely for pleasure. In spite of this, people's inner pressures remain strong and it is not unusual for a couple to feel love for their unborn child before it is even conceived. This is the kind of love which could enrich the lives of children who are offered for adoption. There is always a deep need within men and women either to have children of their own or to adopt. Yet adoption is now fairly infrequent, as there are simply too few children available.

What is the current relationship of law and abortion?

As the ethical controversy rages, society has become engulfed by scientific and medical considerations to such a degree that the Gospel's truths have been ignored. Instead, the world is perceived to be at a watershed in human development and on the brink of a whole new era of achievement. So instead of struggling with moral issues based on the Ten Commandments which have

109

sustained western society so well for many centuries, people have chosen instead to join the chorus of debate on new moral issues such as surrogate motherhood, in-vitro fertilisation, frozen embryos, egg, sperm or embryo donation and so on. Endless official boards of inquiry and commissions attract enormous media coverage and successfully avoid the fact that burgeoning scientific research is straining public moral attitudes.

There is a passive acceptance that scientists have the right to probe into every aspect of human development, but little thought is given to the danger posed to the moral balance. Yet scientists are insistent that they are not trying to create life, but rather are finding out about it. Nevertheless, the inability of the general public to absorb the full implications of recent scientific achievement is becoming more apparent day by day. This passivity in the face of dazzling revelations about science and human reproduction is leading to an imbalance in human thought which politicians and doctors fail to heed. Great harm has been done by television programmes about science where fact-gathering exercises provide no values or moral context, instead leaving the viewer with the impression that science provides the answer to all ills.

Behind all this activity lies a desire for a world population policy under which governments may cajole nations into producing more or fewer children using their political power and without reference to any moral theology or the need of the individual. Decisions of enormous ethical importance are being made for us, and the population is not questioning what is happening for fear of being made to look foolish.

Somewhere, somehow, we need a revolution in the way we view human conception. These days, any woman who wants a child is expected to present the state with a perfectly formed infant. She is offered a whole battery of tests during her pregnancy to safeguard this aim. The concept of a 'seek-and-destroy' policy which would hunt down and kill any child which might be born with a handicap is no fabrication. There is a very real danger that many women will become determined never to conceive at all, because the state's intrusive presence in their personal lives makes the conception of a child seem a threat to their stability rather than a joy which can transform their lives.

110

14

The deterioration of reproductive health and responsibility

The price of ignorance

Few realise how simple Jesus' ministry really was. He was prepared to speak, quietly and gently, to the needs of the whole person, body, mind, spirit and soul. One wonders how he achieved this 'open' approach in the midst of vast crowds of people. To meet such a man ministering today would probably come as a shock. We now associate illness with the nurses in attendance, doctors, consultants and most of all a hygienic, sterilised environment. In the twentieth century, Jesus could easily be dismissed as a charlatan. What would he say to women and men who want to keep their youth, health and sexual appetites?

The two main problems which modern society has failed to address are those of sexual activity and fertility. It is easy to give in to the strong and aggressive emotions of lust, vanity and greed, but the price is high. For 40 years, world population experts and drug manufacturers have promoted artificial contraception in all forms while trying to minimise the amount of information available on the side effects.

Women are often only too keen to control their fertility in the interests of their careers. Some seek eternal youth through the use of hormone replacement therapy, and do not look closely at the pills which promise what they want. The general practitioner is accorded full trust. But what happens if a friend suddenly dies of a stroke or develops cancer? Regrettably, no connection with the Pill is ever discussed publicly. But there has been a surge in the number of deaths among women who ought to be in the prime of life, as many parish priests will witness. Yet they find it safer to keep quiet about this growing trend.

What do men expect of women, now that contraception is so widely available? Surely, the assumption is that women are always available for full vaginal intercourse. This attitude is highlighted by the enormous quantity of pornographic literature which is produced. Men have been led to believe that, for their own well-being, they should take advantage of any opportunity to express their sexuality rather than control it. A classic example is the huge pile of pornographic literature which was shipped to the troops serving in the Falklands War. It sparked considerable comment at the time, and the question is raised 'Is it right?'

Men and women are equipped to produce healthy children and grandchildren and may feel the procreation of their dynastic descendants to be their greatest achievement and their strongest sexual instinct. But now there is a public awareness that men and women are victims of a huge programme which has backfired on society. We have not yet reached the point where we blame big business tycoons who are cashing in on the tender sexuality of teenagers, but it is not far off.

Birth control experts now call for ever younger children to be drawn into their programme of sex education. They have won the support of Government, whose members are worried at the increasing teenage pregnancy rate. As a result, teenagers are encouraged to use post-coitally inserted intra-uterine devices or the Morning-After Pill, which induce early abortion. These desperate measures reflect a deteriorating environment, in which there is surely too much promotion of sexual activity and a falling away of stable family life.

Is it right to encourage young couples to engage in sexual activity before they are physically or emotionally mature? Is it right to push them into situations which they have not the maturity to deal with? Most of all, is it right that young couples who want to experience a stable, married family life should end up helping to bear the multi-billion pound burden of care for one-parent families?

History shows that it is possible to retrieve a stable family outlook, but that such a change would require the introduction of stringent laws, requiring women to represent a stabilising force to their children and husbands, and the promotion of marriage. Most of all, women would be encouraged to bear a responsibility for the care of their children into adulthood, rather than trying to maintain their own careers. Most women know in their hearts that there is no tranquillity in trying to ride two horses: motherhood and career. But twentieth century society dictates otherwise. Women are capable of succeeding both in their careers, and in motherhood, but nobody has considered the huge stress involved in trying to do both. The situation can be even more complex if women use hormone-based contraceptives which can upset the natural balance of their bodies, so intermittently giving rise to further complications.

Artificial contraceptives and their alternatives

Has anyone yet provided a well-rounded view of the strengths and weaknesses of the various contraceptive aids on offer? Are those who promote natural family planning now in a stronger position, or are their options still taking a back seat? Although the world needs a broader outlook on contraception, the failure of governments to enforce morality through law necessarily narrows the debate. Few are prepared to enter a debate about whether sexual morality should be favoured. Such a debate would open up a minefield, as the powerful drug companies would try to upset proceedings at the earliest opportunity. But the media officially offer a platform for the people's views. If they can give such liberal coverage to the Warnock and Gillick sagas, they should also be able to apply themselves to testing the public's views on day-to-day issues. If ours is a democratic society which allows free speech, why is its diversity of views not reflected in the media?

There are many apparently irreconcilable differences of opinion on all the key issues presented by contraception, but people currently have no opportunity to reach a reflective and informed conclusion. Many are wary of confronting a sliding scale of values which has developed during the past four decades. A jury system of 'twelve good men and true' might reach an unbiased judgement. Once again, however, standards have slipped, and the jury system is now regularly subject to close scrutiny – a fact which reveals a lack of trust in the judiciary system that is subsequently amplified by newspaper, radio and television journalists. When Victoria Gillick took the Department of Health and Social Security to court to challenge its advice to doctors to give contraceptive advice and treatment to young girls, would a jury have given her the benefit of the doubt?

Mrs Gillick wanted to ban a leaflet being circulated to doctors which contained information on how to give contraceptive advice without parental consent to girls under 16 years of age. She failed in her attempt, but in the course of the debate, two interesting facts emerged. Firstly, Mrs Gillick and the DHSS had very different ideas about the factual consequences that might result from the alternative legal options offered in the field of contraceptive advice for teenagers. Secondly, the two sides held very diverse outlooks on moral values. In spite of an extensive debate on the issue, little or no attention was given to Mrs Gillick's proposal of an alternative approach to teenagers. This alternative was the Ovarian Monitoring Method, which was developed following research by Professor James Brown in Melbourne, Australia and Professor Erik Odeblad of Umce, Sweden.

The Ovarian Monitoring Method enables a woman to measure her oestrogen and progesterone levels throughout her cycle, so that she can identify the time of ovulation and fertility. Since 1968, when the method was first taught outside Australia, its use has spread to more than 100 countries by means of one-to-one instruction of couples and international conferences.

After 30 years of research into the structure of cervical mucus. Professor Odeblad can interpret the mucus patterns and their significance in relation to sperm functions and conception. He is firmly of the opinion that synthetic hormones damage the cervix, and that the Pill may cause infertility. The greatest recommendation of this ovulation method is that it requires no drugs or devices, but rather an awareness of the changing mucus and the application of that knowledge (*The Billings Method* by Dr Evelyn Billing and associates, p208).

Many people try to challenge this method of contraception, but the scientific facts are indisputable. Its weak point is that it relies on self-control, and therefore is susceptible to human emotions. But for those couples who are calm, loving and orderly, it has been found safe, reliable and easy to use. The bonus of this approach is that it hands full control to the couple, and often results in a deep sense of satisfaction as they tune in to the natural rhythm of their bodies.

Responsibility for reproductive health

Family planning, or the control of conception, is an essential part of human reproduction, since ideally every child conceived should be wanted by its parents. Sadly, this is not always the case, despite the fact that the availability of artificial contraceptive aids is apparent everywhere. In the UK, the National Health Service accepts responsibility for the provision of a comprehensive service for the control of conception. The Family Planning Association alone has more than 1,000 clinics, and there are also clinics run by local authorities and hospitals.

Nevertheless, the ethos surrounding the sexual act is very different from that prevailing just 100 years ago. Society no longer tries merely to prevent conception; it now aims to exert absolute control. From the medical point of view, certain conditions may provide a temporary or permanent threat to the health of a woman should she become pregnant, and in these cases avoidance of pregnancy is vital. But the number of women affected is surprisingly few. When advising on contraception, medical practitioners tend to be hesitant until a method is chosen; only then will they advise on the possible medical or psychological effects of using it. They see a woman's sexual activity as entirely her own affair.

This official cautious approach can contrast with the strong views held by many people about their chosen method of contraception and contraception as a whole. Unfortunately, there are risks in every form of medication, and there are risks inherent in taking oral steroid contraceptive pills, yet pure statistics show that oral contraceptives are the most effective and the safest form of contraception.

So who, in this decision-making process, is responsible for reproductive health? The Government? The medical profession? Global population policy-makers? The answer, perhaps, is that each person makes his or her own decision, using the free will which is innate to every man and woman. Yet even this free will needs direction and control, for the good of humanity.

It seems there is no watertight policy in existence because human nature is so wilful. Currently, society balances its moral intuition against its conceptions of liberty and equality. Contemporary law now sets a minimum standard of behaviour which still leaves many people dissatisfied. Where does one go from here?

Perhaps this is when we should turn to our own consciences. We should bear in mind the fact that men have killed in good conscience for the sake of an ideology, to combat a heresy and so on. Jesus warned his disciples of this weakness: 'Indeed the time is coming when anyone who kills you will think he is doing a holy service for God.' (John 16:2) It is apparent that when we do not inform our consciences, they will not direct us towards the character and will of God.

The responsibility of the word 'No'

Has the public ever held an informed and educated debate on when and where to use the word 'No' in relation to moral dilemmas? The said public would probably be rather bewildered by the question. Nobody expects to make responsible decisions by issuing a straightforward refusal of whatever is on offer. This is obvious in the endless committees which run the population's lives through debate. Because there is now a high standard of education, turning down any option is not seen as an adequate response. So if law and morality are to prosper, everybody needs to contribute to the debate.

It is easy to overlook the hold that the media have on the public. Most people credit themselves with holding strong independent opinions which they have thought out themselves, but how true can that be, when most people watch several hours of television a day? A television screen in the home is like a resident moral guide, a monitoring device which might sound a warning note if any deviation from a perceived standard occurs. In the UK, the BBC is perceived as the upholder of standards, while independent television channels are not. Cable and satellite channels give access to a wide variety of programmes, all of which may reflect a different range of moral standards. Television helps its audience to rebel against inherited instincts and gives it arguments with which to reject them. Free will is now nothing better than a lax conscience with which other people can do as they will. Few are willing to give Christ the lead, and be obedient to His signals in order to resist this pressure on minds and actions.

Every person has experienced the effectiveness of the word 'No' from early childhood. However much it may be rejected or argued against, it is rare that the original impulse can be changed. Once it has been uttered, its verdict cannot be altered unless pressurised.

Unfortunately, conscience is no respecter of person, and it makes itself felt regardless of the highest authorities which might confront it. But who is prepared to follow their conscience, particularly in relation to reproductive health? Christ's disciples, Peter and John, were very clear where they stood when they were challenged by the rulers of Jerusalem about their right to preach the word of God. Are we prepared to echo their words? 'You must judge whether in God's eyes it is right to listen to you and not to God. We cannot stop proclaiming what we have seen and heard.' (Acts 4: 19,20)

15

Sex and Christ's traditional teaching

Sex and holiness

When the children of Israel left Egypt in search of the promised land, God dwelt with them and provided for their needs in the desert as they moved from being a nomadic people to being a holy nation. Moses, their leader, was able to hear the spoken word of God, and it was through him that God revealed the code which was to govern their hearts and actions.

This code was the Ten Commandments, where all duties and obligations to God and to each other are spelled out. The books of Leviticus and Deuteronomy were later written to spell out how these commandments were to be applied in everyday life. The first section of Deuteronomy deals with the Israelites' relationship with God, while the second is concerned with personal conduct and behaviour within a holy calling. This Levitical Code concentrates on matters which may render a person defiled, and describes the procedures necessary to make a person acceptable for worship. Certain sexual activities are forbidden, such as incest, homosexuality and sexual activity outside marriage.

Many people interpret the Book of Leviticus as a programme of health and hygiene, though it may also be seen as descriptions of the steps necessary to perform religious ceremonies. Many theories have been put forward over the centuries, but one refrain from the book remains widespread: 'Cleanliness is next to godliness.' The Israelites insisted on clean food, air, water, clothes and houses. The book gives careful instructions for the disposal of sewage, the burial of the dead and the control of infectious diseases. Even a twentieth-century student is often amazed at the clarity of instruction contained in the book of Leviticus.

God made a promise which he asked his chosen people to believe. His words to Moses when he entered the desert of Sinai could apply to modern society: 'If you listen to the voice of Yahweh your God and do what he regards as right, if you pay attention to his commandments and keep all his laws, I shall never inflict on you any of the diseases that I inflicted on the Egyptians, for I am Yahweh your Healer.' (Exodus 17:26)

How much illness could be avoided today if people followed the Leviticus code of health? Behind all the instructions is a cleansing process which has a spiritual significance. For example, if one looks at the distinction between creatures which were clean and those which were unclean, it is startling to realise that despite all the twentieth-century regulations, poultry meat can carry salmonella.

In fact, God is concerned about purity and holiness. Even the uncleanliness surrounding childbirth served a purpose, because it meant that a woman who had recently given birth could have a set period of time on her own to recover before taking up her normal everyday duties in society. In the same context, menstruation and seminal emission also had to be controlled for the good of the community. The uniqueness of conception and pregnancy reflected God's holiness, and any child made in his image bore the mark of holiness. Mosaic law tried to ensure that a holy people could dwell in harmony with God, with holiness as a way of life rather than an extra.

When St Paul spoke to the people of Corinth, he brought the Israelites firmly under the teaching of Jesus, quoting directly from the Old Testament: 'I shall fix my home among them, I will be their God and they will be my people. Get away from them, purify yourselves, says the Lord. Do not touch anything unclean and then I shall welcome you.' (2 Corinthians 6: 16,17)

Women are hazy about the details of pregnancy, but not about the sexual act. Yet they are vulnerable because they have not been taught about the reality and holiness of conception and the discomfort and mental strain that accompany pregnancy. All this stress may be swept aside once the baby has been delivered safely, and any new mother feels an enormous sense of achievement. Yet women are not encouraged to realise that even before birth, the child she is carrying is a reality, uniquely made. The uniqueness of childbearing is only fully realised after the difficulties and trauma of childbirth and the painful journey taken by the child through the pelvic girdle into the outside world. In all the distress of childbirth, a new-born child can reflect a transcendent purity which reveals that it is a child of God.

Christ's teaching about the family

If Christ had met Sigmund Freud (1865-1939), what would he have said about the Austrian psychiatrist's theories? Would he have argued, reasoned, become angry, or bewildered? Or would he have responded simply by showing God's love? I have no doubt that Christ would have challenged Freud's belief that religious belief is no more than a projection of a child's relationship with its parents which is engendered by the stresses of life. Could Freud ever have been brought to believe that the conscience is an inherent part of human nature, not imposed from outside?

What is indisputable is that Freud's theories had profound consequences on the teaching of sexual evolution. He taught that the repression of infantile sexuality lies at the root of adult neuroses. From this, he developed his theory of the Oedipus complex, a label coined by Freud for the unconscious antagonism of a son towards the father who represented a rival for the mother's affection. Where a girl was antagonistic towards her mother, the rival for her father's attention, Freud called it the Electra complex. Freud taught that sexuality was a universal part of human development that ought to resolve itself in most children in late childhood.

This interpretation of children's development shelved problems about the origin of moral values, and put all responsibility on the influence of parents on their children. Denying the existence of absolute moral values and the existence of God, humanists won widespread respect for their belief that the standard by which the conscience makes its judgements should be freely and openly modified by outside influences, including the state, and developed to fit the plans of the individual or society. The fact that a chosen moral frame of reference can vary from one individual or social group to another presents us with an outlook that can easily be seen to endanger the values and standards of a Christian morality and faith which is based on the character and will of God.

Matters have not been helped by the huge strides made in medical knowledge, and the public is all the more vulnerable to the ethical conflict that has resulted. Most people believe they need not get involved in the debate, but in fact no one can escape. The conflicts that have arisen around the issues of abortion on demand, controlled infanticide and euthanasia should prompt profound unease. The general public is increasingly bewildered by the many shades of opinion expressed by medical experts, and is hesitant to make any judgement. Yet the abandonment of Christian principles within society does cause disquiet, and no one who exerts any authority within their own families can avoid becoming involved in these socio-political problems.

It is time to sharpen up our dulled consciences, which have lost their edge as legal protection for the family has been eroded. Most people accept that they need to live by an ethical code of conduct, but to promote one particular code to the general public could open them up to attack. Christians need once again to look afresh at the Christian interpretation of ethics which is enshrined in the individual conscience, is sensitive to right and wrong, and is accountable to God.

Christ's mother Mary, who received God's gift of Himself two thousand years ago, can help us. Jesus used to go to Jerusalem with his parents every year to celebrate the Passover. When just 12 years old, he had developed sufficient will of his own to stay behind and challenge the teachers in the temple. Mary and Joseph placed such trust in their son that it did not cross their minds that he would not have travelled with them on the journey back to Nazareth.

Imagine the agony of Mary and Joseph when they realised that their extraordinary son could distance himself from them to the extent of disobeying them. Most people have friends or relatives who have experienced the same realisation. Jesus, who was both fully human and fully divine, was pulled in two directions. On the one hand, he was a gifted child who was carefully brought up and protected by his parents. On the other hand, God had given him a special calling. In some ways, it must have been almost a relief to Jesus finally to be able to challenge the learned teachers in the temple. Like all gifted boys, he had reached a point where he wanted to explore and debate with like-minded people. He was so carried away that he almost reprimanded his mother when she said how worried she had been. 'Why were you looking for me? Did you not know that I must be in my Father's house?' (Luke 2:49) His comment must have amazed and bewildered his parents. It was as if the son they knew so well was suddenly showing a side of himself they had never seen before.

Yet Jesus, a boy who probably had sufficient intelligence and knowledge to have wandered off to fend for himself, was ready to acknowledge openly that his parents had a natural authority over him. He would not have been a participant in the Children's Crusade in 1212 when parties of children as young as 11 from France and western Germany gathered together after the disastrous failure of the Fourth Crusade (1202-04) and set out to capture Jerusalem. Instead, Jesus submitted to his parents' authority, living in obedience to God and man. Not until he was 30 did he start his ministry. Until then, it seems he lived in harmony with his parents. Essentially, these early years were a time of preparation of which very little is known. There is sufficient in the Gospels to show how Mary was also preparing herself for his ministry. Mary's courage as a mother is an example to all women. She was ready to live totally for God, centring her whole life around Jesus who was to die on the cross at Calvary.

Mary offers a prototype of family life in which order prevailed through love, teaching and interpretation of Holy Scripture. Equally, Mary was the prototype of the Christian Church, which still strives to fit, as she did, into God's plan. Jesus was conceived by the Holy Spirit through Mary. The power of the Holy Spirit continues to be realised in the lives of Christians and the Church so that they can all come together in the body of Christ. The Bible is full of examples of family life that illustrate the blessings of obedience and the dangers of disobediences and which can be applied today to family, Church or nation.

Sex, Christ and the nuclear family

The media offers an abundance of reports on the disintegration of family life, but few are ready to face up to the Christian way of life which forms the cornerstone of western family life. In fact, most people are contented to sit back and watch the attacks on family life and the feminist movement in the belief that these forces are irresistable. Now, funding from Brussels and from Westminster is available to groups who want to continue to attack Christian values. Activists hold key posts on research bodies, committees and charities concerned with children. In fact, in some instances employers have been so indoctrinated that they actively seek out single parents to join their work-force in preference to individuals who are single, chaste and upright in outlook.

Even people from comfortable middle-class backgrounds are not afraid to collect the supportive and compensatory resources provided by the state to enable them to flee the family home, whether employed or not. Young men frequently express their fury at seeing their role as wage-earner and protector of the family being so eroded. Yet research with established couples shows how strongly marriage affects a man's approach to his work. After marriage, he works harder to improve the conditions and experience of family life. Even so, there is little or no support for the traditional role of the male as provider. Rather, there has been a systematic erosion of men's earning power, which means they are often unable to support their families purely on their own salaries.

In the field of embryo research, so much progress has been made in the mechanics of conceiving and carrying a child, such as IVF, donated eggs and sperm, and many other permutations.

But where does this research leave family life and motherhood? Who is the mother in a situation where a woman provides an egg fertilised by her husband to be carried by a surrogate mother? Is there motherhood in the woman who carries the child, even though she is not related genetically?

A further area of research has opened up in cryology, where scientists have discovered how to freeze fertilised eggs or embryos and store them indefinitely. In fact, it is feasible that a surrogate mother might only not carry a child commissioned by its parents, but that she would play host to a thawed embryo from an embryo bank. This Orwellian culture is no longer science fiction: it is here with us.

Pope John Paul II noted the change in society when he commented: 'The world has largely lost respect for human life from the moment of conception. The world is weak in upholding the indissoluble unit of marriage. It fails to support the stability and holiness of family life. There is a crisis of truth and responsibility in human relationships.' In fact, Christians are failing to listen to their consciences. Jesus Christ became incarnate of the Holy Spirit and was born of the Virgin Mary, so giving an example for all subsequent generations – including those who think that example no longer applies.

Today's high-tech interference with reproduction has produced acrimony, arguments and endless confusion. Many people hope that a middle ground will develop. But is this likely when people are unable to cope with their increased sexual activity or control their fertility in line with their Christian inheritance? The words of Pope John Paul II offer a rare hope and as Pope of a global village, he deserves a response.

16

Grandmothers and the contraceptive revolution

Inheritance

Grandparents, or ageing parents, can talk with some authority – based on experience – about their memories of the vicious poor and the correlation between crime and degrading poverty found in slums or appalling housing conditions. Such poverty is no longer to be found in the United Kingdom, yet these same people are horrified when they see replicas of those remembered poor stalking apparently respectable suburbs. They are unwilling to admit their acute discomfort at the way a new wave of crime has appeared in an affluent society. Many wonder where things went wrong, particularly when they themselves have witnessed such remarkable improvements in the material comfort around them. Yet juvenile delinquency has increased even in areas with a high standard of living.

Few would confess that in the general confusion caused by weakening moral standards, the social cohesion offered by traditional social patterns is no long so apparent. There is a tendency to cast the blame elsewhere, on government officials, religious groups or others. But there is no justification for such accusations. At the heart of their distress is the change in their material surroundings which has brought an abrupt end to the community spirit of the past. The fact is, that not many people see their neighbours on a regular basis. One can hardly exaggerate the part the introduction of the motor car has played in human relationships.

Although strong efforts have been made by determined groups in many cities to overcome this influence of the motor car, and many local government policies no longer try to uproot traditional neighbourhoods and communities, the damage has been done during the 50 years during which the motor industry has developed unhindered. Today, many families have been decanted into new housing areas in which they live insular lives, isolated from the many other families who live around them. This development has led to emotional frustration and a breakdown of trust which can easily develop into an aggressive defiance of wider society. There is a tendency to try to support families in this situation rather than seeking to re-establish the traditional social attitudes which have been so disrupted by experimental politics and a surfeit of material comforts.

The true reasons for this new wave of crime lie deep down in women's consciousness, but few care to delve so deep. It is easier to avoid the personal revelations which would doubtless ensue. This refusal to accept the consequences of the changed pattern of living is nowhere more apparent than in the response to any challenge of the contraceptive revolution which has altered the very structure of relationships between women and men. Today, when the word 'sanctity' is used to describe marriage and home life, it is greeted with an involuntary shudder.

The key to a happier existence is held by the numerous women who have themselves benefited from the security of orderly and balanced homes where there has been a social and moral structure. Yet such women are hesitant of offering the authority of experience to alleviate the unhappiness they see in their children, grandchildren or great-grandchildren. Such hesitation is understandable, particularly today, when many lonely old people see their families too involved with their own lives to pay them much attention. It is all too easy for them to feel vulnerable, lost and unsure of what, if any, pressure they should exert.

These people could help to cure society's malaise, but they need considerable courage. Whatever their embarrassment or anxieties, nothing should blind them to the eternal difference between right and wrong, or cause them to shrink from their responsibilities to their descendants. How many women who have seen the results of the contraceptive revolution are ready to admit that women world-wide have been caught up in one of the most ambitious and large-scale experiments ever undertaken? How many will confess that this revolution and the demands of the unisex approach to life have left their children and grand-children searching in vain for the opportunity to be loved and wanted?

How should one define this force known as motherhood? In recent years, numerous people have not received an inherited trust and knowledge of that force because the very role of the mother has been downgraded over the past decades. People like to think that because women have always lived in a culture dominated by men, they should now use recent technological advances to break into the 'cosy' world of men and exert their authority in traditionally male spheres. The struggle over who should control female biological reproduction has had profound implications for women. In the course of the struggle, mother-hood has come to be interpreted as a biological urge which responds only to a pregnancy.

Numerous women want to dispense with the traditional view that motherhood represents the primary sexual and social role for the female. Instead, they condemn this outlook as the result of repressive Victorian morality, where motherhood was the sole and biologically ordained purpose of women's existence, and where wives were economically and sexually subject to their husbands' will.

This limited view is far from the truth. Motherhood taps into a love which reaches into the unplumbed depths of a woman's psyche. Modern psychology describes it as an integrated blending of two psychic principles: firstly, the animus, the intelligible principle of analysis, enables critical reflection, controls and calculates; secondly, the anima, which is defined as the theme of relationships, communion and unity. The anima, or psyche, being the soul, makes contact with God and forms a fem-inine relationship with God. Through the example of Mary and her feminine powers of contemplation, women can ultimately reach an understanding of their role as potential bearers of children.

127

Christians need to accept that the feminine role is characterised not just by its receptivity (or even a rebellious acceptance) but also by the ability to respond and surrender itself in loving obedience. Christ's mother showed when she conceived and bore the Son of God what was possible when submitting to the Word of God. Today, the influence of contraception is causing the disintegration of families and drawing mothers away from their homes. Often, mothers are simply not there to exert this quality of sanctity – that strange unseen force through which women 'tune in' to being mothers.

Numerous men and women with many years' experience in family care will relate how at first they marvelled at the new opportunities for young couples to control their reproduction. Today, however, they are anxious as matters have not turned out as smoothly as had been expected.

Society can and should acknowledge openly that alongside the introduction of the Pill and other drugs controlling reproduction, enormous strides have been made in all aspects of economic and material standards. Yet these changes have engendered a restlessness across all levels of society. The Victorians talked earnestly about the social effects of modern industrial techniques and the growth of town populations, but they did not understand how those changes bring about the breakdown of natural order. Townspeople often have little or no understanding of the countryside or of nature's life cycle.

It is easy to feel nervous when confronting the forces around us which are breaking up what family life there is, and which are undermining any residual respect for marriage as the cornerstone of home life. But people are faced with a simple choice: to opt for the narrow discipline of trying to make the lots of certain people easier and happier, or to spread the task wider and try to shore up the family against those influences which are threatening its strength and stability.

Today, young women who have the advantage of a contraceptive control over their own bodies both inside and outside marriage, are often apprehensive at the thought of marriage for a lifetime. Marriage is an obligation, and as such calls for sacrifices. Unfortunately, state legislators have not seen fit to maintain the institution of marriage through the authority handed down to them through the centuries to care for the helpless and underprivileged. In fact, the state's recent recognition of relationships between 'partners' has contributed to the breakdown of traditional order.

The law of the land is now so geared that children are taught about contraception before puberty. Children are also protected from child abuse and battering. Who is right? Surely it is in the state's interests to strengthen the sense of responsibility entailed by marriage, and to support the sacrificial role which is to be found in maintaining a marriage. Instead, the erosion of state support for marriage is weakening the very social values which governments aim to strengthen. Yet the family unit on which so much of society is based constitutes more than a mere social and economic unit. It is a community of love and solidarity which is independently developed in each grouping to teach and transmit cultural, social, spiritual and religious values which are essential for the development and well-being of society.

Sadly, humanity has been let down by people's attitudes to freedom and the misuse of free will. True freedom is not about claiming rights; it is about responsibilities and duties. Today, that freedom can easily come under the control of independent men or groups who try and concentrate too much power in their own hands. This trend has developed to such a degree that people feel they are missing out on a deep sense of justice, good will and public service, and that they are abandoning fundamental convictions. Essentially, this was part of the Albigensian movement when there was an abandonment of motherhood by women who sought to follow this heretical sect.

History shows that the character of a nation is formed in homes through parental example rather than in schools and institutions. The widespread respect for Mothering Sunday shown by mothers and children alike shows a residual awareness of this fact among the public. In fact, it is called mid-Lent Sunday or *Mi-carême,* after Isaiah's words, now used at the beginning of the Eucharist: 'Rejoice ye with Jerusalem.' (Isaiah 16:10) Could it be that children and young mothers once again want the reassurance of love, pure love, in their lives – the love which the children of the

129

Children's Crusade found they lacked after the Albigensian movement when mothers abandoned their roles as wives, mothers and home-makers?

Once again, we must listen to those whose lives lie ahead of them, and who demand our love and attention. On Mothering Sunday, the Church wants to draw the attention of the congregation to the example of the Mother-Church and the Holy Family, but over the centuries this outlook has evolved into a belief that Mothering Sunday offers an opportunity to say thank-you to mothers for their love.

Grandparents and their attitude to contraception

One of the hardest things for the older generation to accept is the concept of a man and woman sharing equal status within a marriage. The effects of this development are profound and far-reaching. So many talk boldly about the changed relationship between the sexes, both of whom now have the vote and equal rights to employment in any profession. This process has developed so much momentum that most people believe it cannot be halted until the battle for equality has been fully won. Most grandparents see that this dramatic change cannot be reversed, so they accept the results: suffering children from broken homes, second or common-law marriages which shatter the continuity of families, the destabilisation of human relationships and most of all the violation of established conventions which has thrown community life into confusion.

Few, if any, understand the changed status of marriage which lies at the heart of this shift in attitude. 'I feel I am skipping two generations when I talk to my parents about marriage,' commented one young woman.

I believe that the contraceptive revolution underpins the changed understanding of relationships, but once again, everybody, particularly the older generation, avoid mentioning the subject when talking about their families. To do so would mean admitting to themselves the disturbance within their own lives caused by the moral outlook of their children or grandchildren.

Marriage itself has always been surrounded by a veil of privacy, and incredible myths and misconceptions have grown up around it. Young people see falling in love as easy, because it leads directly to co-habitation and from there to a regular relationship. Older people understand falling in love as courtship, engagement and eventually marriage, usually without a trial period of co-habitation.

Today, when so many marriages fail, the breakdown of the family network can easily prompt a live-and-let-live attitude towards the attendant problems that can result, and this in itself has encouraged the collapse of traditional ways of thought and action.

Two serious questions need to be asked: Is being in love the basic ingredient of a happy marriage? Is the traditional heterosexual relationship, where the woman takes second place to the man, practicable any more?

In this debate, most people ignore the fact that the younger generations have been inundated with talk and representations of sex. All forms of the media have discussed and presented creative and recreational sex from every angle. The result is that young people are bored by sex. That boredom is barely noted by those who believe that there is an insatiable appetite for more and more media coverage of sex.

As a result, one frequently meets young men or women who have experienced the basic act of sexual intercourse, and who understand marriage simply to be a sexual partnership with one other person for life, rather than a full relationship.

The older generation should humbly admit that the achievement of a lifelong relationship of love and friendship is a tough assignment, requiring considerable acts of sacrifice from both participants in order for the marriage to develop and remain stable. Unfortunately, we can become guilty of using the excitement around the love-life of a daughter or son to start feeling dissatisfied with our wives or husbands, and want the same excitement that we see our children enjoying.

Society has also failed people who have been led to believe that contraceptives can be used within a marriage or in an extra-marital sexual relationship without any physical or psychological side effects. A full discussion of the skills involved in living together in love and friendship often fails to take place because so much importance is attached to sexual activity between the partners at the expense of all other aspects of the relationship. Without the discipline of marriage, the use of contraceptives can result in a progressive alienation and a rapid decision that the couple are not suited.

It is not good enough simply to dismiss the problems by saying that marriage is now a completely different proposition from the traditional concept. Many researchers talk about the exciting development of the new type of relationship between men and women that is destined to shape the twenty-first century and facilitate the coming of age of biological sciences. Little attention, if any, is paid to what is going on at ground level. People ignore the fact that young women are increasingly dying from illnesses brought on by the stress of sexual equality, the strain of trying to continue a professional career while also acting as wife, mother and home-maker. In at least one hospice movement in Colchester, Essex, a new wing has recently been opened to cater for bereaved children whose mothers have died and whose fathers may have abandoned them.

Young women are frightened. Those who want to stay at home and look after their husbands and children know that that is all they can do. Yet relatives, friends, neighbours, in fact any acquaintance, will always say after the birth of a child: 'So, when are you going back to work?' Many new mothers have meekly tried to earn an income while being housewives and looking after their children. While there are usually apparently good reasons for taking this course of action, in their hearts their unacknowledged desire is to devote themselves entirely to their homes and families. The new father, if he really loves his offspring, will use his authority to encourage his wife to stay at home, but he will always feel nervous and vulnerable in an age where his outlook is not considered rational.

Behind all natural desires is the wish to be loved and honoured, and this can be achieved by couples offering each other an assurance and honour on which a lifelong tie can be formed. The state and church leaders appear to have lost sight of the basic fact that *marriage exists to provide a guarantee that the duties of parenthood will be faithfully discharged by both parties.* Those who fail to support marriage and make themselves sexually available outside marriage are betraying their own motherhood and fatherhood, for they are shirking the joint responsibility of rearing a child from infancy into adulthood.

The way ahead

The solution is so simple that it hurts. The following story is an illustration. A woman who was infertile adopted a boy and a girl and considered herself a lucky woman. She exerted a firm discipline over the boy, and he delighted his parents. The daughter, however, opposed her parents at every opportunity. Nevertheless, her parents struggled on, and they were not surprised when she had an unplanned baby. But there was no question of leaving her to fend on her own. They loved her and she was their daughter. The grandmother readied herself to bring up another generation, while her daughter when back to work. In time, she fell in love, and became engaged to a boy at work. The courtship was sober, their love honourable and the young couple's relationship progressed alongside their friendship. The marriage took place with a quiet thankfulness that the illegitimate child could be adopted into the marriage. These events took place over several years.

The challenge taken up by this grandmother is one that many elderly people refuse to face. They resent having to give up their increasingly precious time and face the demands of such a situation. These parents were obeying deeply held convictions, yet they are in a minority.

Churches and communities can set up all kinds of organised groups, but if society does not face the damage being done to the family by the sexual revolution, they can only have a limited impact. The soul of family life is under threat, as the widespread use of contraceptives destabilises marriages and makes families into ever larger units through remarriage and other partnerships. Perpetual division within families results in a permanent breakdown of love and trust. Peace can only come by accepting that the spirit and atmosphere of a family, lovingly concerned with each other's welfare, can only grow in grace when the surrounding circumstances allow.

There are many services which offer preventative skills to stop marriages from failing, and there are various different therapies on offer. Yet those in government and in the churches refuse to guide the new generations with inherited Christian ideals.

Now, secular standards dominate political action, particularly in the area of marriage and family life. It is up to the older generations who have experienced a stability handed down by tradition to exert their authority through word and action. Years of experience can bring a realisation of life's priorities, and now is the time for the elderly to reveal their knowledge of the Word and guidance of God in their lives.

17

The answer of Mary, the mother of the Incarnate Word

Who is Mary?

This century has seen the development of liberal theology, where researchers have tried to define culture and civilisation in relation to God's purpose. So at times, as science has developed, traditional teaching about the position of Mary, the mother of God, has been challenged. People have been busy fashioning God and the world to conform to their own tastes and have moved away from the contemplative approach to God. Even Catholics, who have maintained a constant devotion to Mary over the centuries, have developed diverse opinions in order to fall in line with the present-day outlook.

A massive Marian movement has developed in many parts of the world. Mary can be seen as a 'masterpiece' of the Holy Spirit, who surrendered herself in love and obedience to serve God's Word. Yet for some reason, people are not happy to go along with the Orthodox viewpoint, under which nothing can be achieved without the blessing and intercession of the Mother of God. In fact, the love of the Orthodox for Mary can be described as child-like in their trustful belief in her constant protection and inter-cessions. She is the mother of all people on earth, and, as a moth-er, she cannot refuse to listen to her children's cries for help and need for protection.

The Orthodox have a calm and quiet acceptance of Mary. In Roman Catholicism, there is a certain excited undertone to the veneration of Mary, who is both prophet and intercessor. Yet, when she makes her appearances to visionaries, she constantly urges Christians to engage in family prayer, fasting, confession and regular worship. Underpinning all her teaching is the need for peace, particularly in family life.

Mary herself was conceived of human parents, and then by extraordinary means was lifted up to a position which has dominated the Christian Church for 2,000 years through her virginal conception of Jesus Christ. During this time, her unique example has been explored in the most minute detail. Yet throughout there have been those who have jeered, disbelieved and ridiculed. Indeed, given the opposition, Mary should by rights have disappeared from the Christian calendar. But this has not happened.

Instead, over the years, numerous titles have been bestowed on the Virgin Mary. The most prevalent one is Mother of God. This title alone must cause Christians to pause and think, because it implies a recognition of holiness which cannot be attributed to any other human being. Mary's maternal status is made clear in the first offices of the Church. The Roman Creed, which appeared at the end of the second century, shows that her status was established during the age of the Apostles. It begins 'I believe in God, the Father Almighty, and in Christ Jesus, His only son, our Lord, who was born from the Holy Ghost and the Virgin Mary.' Later, the last part was changed to '...our Lord, who was conceived by the Holy Ghost, born of the Virgin Mary.'

Clearly, there were times when people tried to argue against this creed. Nestorius (d. 451), Archbishop of Constantinople, was one of these. He firmly stated that Mary was not the Mother of God and as a result of his belief denied that the human and divine were fully united in Jesus Christ. The maternity of Mary should spur all Christians to consider the question of the Incarnation, especially in view of the fact that Jesus Christ came in human form to redeem the whole of humankind. St Cyril (d. 444), Patriarch of Alexandria, became alarmed when he heard Nestorius state that 'Theotokos' (Mother of God) could not be applied to the Virgin Mary, and that Mary was instead 'the mother of the humanity of Christ'.

St Cyril defended the contested word, and persuaded Pope

136

Celestine (d. 432) to convene a synod in Rome in 430 whose purpose was to excommunicate Nestorius on the grounds of heresy. The excommunication was finally approved by the Council of Ephesus in 431. The Council proclaimed 'If anyone could not confess that Emanuel is truly God, and that in consequence the Blessed Virgin is the Mother of God – for she brought forth according to the flesh, the Word of God made flesh – let him be anathema.'

These stirring words must have resulted in many quiet shakings of heads as people questioned Cyril's methods, but his abilities as a theologian were beyond dispute. Cyril went on to formulate the doctrine systematically, basing it on the teachings of St Athanasius (296-373), former bishop of Alexandria, and the Cappodocian Fathers. The latter were three brilliant leaders of philosophical Christian Orthodoxy who lived in the late fourth century – St Basil the Great, Bishop of Caesarea in Cappodocia; St Gregory, Bishop of Nazianzus and St Gregory, Bishop of Nyssa. Their unity of thought led to the defeat of Arianism, a contemporary powerful heresy which denied the true divinity of Jesus Christ.

Since this early controversy, the Christian churches have been faithful to the doctrine of the full humanity and divinity of Christ. Some of them have justly looked to Mary in their apostolic work, believing that she provides a living example of maternal love which should inspire all those who try to co-operate in the apostolic mission of the Church for the regeneration of men. The example set by the mother of Jesus cannot be avoided and, as the Christian's role model, helps every individual in the Church, at every stage of human life and in every particular Christian vocation.

Why was this woman called into God's service in this way? The question recurs constantly, and the historical records surrounding her life and death are the subject of frequent dispute. The New Testament fails even to give the names of her parents. Yet there was no dispute in the early Church that Mary was the daughter of Anne and Joachim. At the time, people were not prepared to challenge the books of the Old Testament which described the history of salvation and the preparations for the coming of Christ. Mary's central role was foreshadowed by the promise of victory over the serpent which was given to Adam and Eve after their fall into sin (Genesis 3, 15). Surely Mary offers us the New Covenant, and is placed at the centre of salvation and of the Church. Like a spouse, she is surely the mother who will deliver the children of God.

In St Luke's Gospel, the author takes the reader into the company of poor and holy people such as Elizabeth and Zachariah, Anna and Simeon, Joseph and Mary. He reveals Mary's purity as she awaits the delivery of her child, the Messiah. St Luke continues the 'ark of the covenant' theme in his account of Mary's visit to her cousin Elizabeth and the blessing that arose on Zachariah's house where Mary resided for three months, for Luke saw the coming of the new Eve in Mary.

Without doubt, devotion to Mary and belief in the efficacy of her intercession dates from very early Church, and has at times been in danger of becoming a cult. The decisions of the Council of Ephesus gave impetus to the growing veneration of Mary. Yet since the Reformation, any devotion to Our Lady can provoke a strong negative response among Protestants. Mary is needed more than ever at this time of crisis when childbirth and motherhood are surrounded by increasing uncertainty. But how can Mary reach us if Christians are so apprehensive of asking for her prayers and protection?

The Holy Family provides a role model. Christ led a hidden life at Nazareth with Mary and Joseph. Of His 33 years of earthly life, He chose to spend 30 years in silence and obscurity, being obedient and earning His living. This hidden life deserves some reflection on our part. It reflects Christ's filial devotion to God, expressed in a family made up of the three holiest human beings in history. Mary, Joseph and Jesus were united in their daily tasks which they made holy through prayers and meditation, and they sanctified their family life through the domestic virtues of charity, obedience and mutual help. St Luke makes this absolutely clear when he refers to Jesus' life at Nazareth: 'Jesus went down with them [his parents] then and came to Nazareth and lived under their authority. His mother stored up all these things in her heart. And Jesus increased in wisdom, in stature and in favour with God and with people.' (Luke 2:51)

A reflection of the total and unique trust which had been established by Jesus and his parents is revealed in the wedding of Cana, when Jesus' mother expected Jesus to do something when the wedding reception ran out of wine. 'They have no wine,' she told her son, In return, Jesus challenged her: 'Woman, what do you want from me? My hour is not yet come.' Showing a mother's intuition, which most people have experienced at some stage, Mary took no notice of his protest, and told the servants 'Do whatever he tells you.' After miraculously turning the water into wine, Jesus once again travelled with his mother, his brothers and friends to Capernaum. But the astonishment of the bridegroom can still teach the reader of the Bible, as he exclaimed: 'Everybody serves good wine first and the worse wine when the guests are well wined; but you have kept the best wine till now.' (John 2, 11)

Indeed, God has helped us to understand the path He wants us to tread on the road to our salvation, but the grace shown in His readiness to work with women to produce children made in His image still defies our understanding. Many Christians are like the guests at that wedding feast. Although as Christians we are filled with the Holy Spirit at our conception, we have become dull and stupefied by an abundance of poor wine, we should now be reaching out for a renewal of thought and action, provided by Christ, as we seek fresh wine to fill the vessels of salvation.

Christians struggle with Mary's example and the challenge posed by Jesus' conception and birth to a virgin and single mother. The current world-wide debate about the value of a person's life therefore arouses strong feelings and passionate assertions. Yet the answer to all this distress is contained in the message of the Incarnation.

One question which now provokes great anger is whether women are appropriate carriers of the sacramental and symbolic role of priest. Many people, whether theologically trained or not, are quick to point out the pastoral ministry which women can exert. By their very femininity they can use their gifts of sympathy, compassion and warmth for the benefits of others. The idea that women already have a vocation, placed on them by a loving Father at conception, is not allowed. Yet the female embryo in the womb already holds all the eggs for any future conception. The ministry of women is to bear fruit to a child or children, and, if this is not possible, at least to exert their motherhood in caring for those around them.

A woman's vocation is placed on her by her very femininity. Only when she denies this does a sudden spiritual yearning appear for an alternative, such as priesthood. Only in the example of Mary can women find hope and happiness and it is to her that women of every age should look for inspiration and illumination when they want to do God's will. She is unique of all her sex, but (and it is a big 'but') she shows humanity the distinctive values of humility and obedience – the same values which are being trodden underfoot by feminist dogma.

Mary's quiet presence and influence in her Son's ministry shows us that her motherhood was always there for Him, showing a humanity in her humility which evidenced a great depth of prayer. Somehow, she always seemed to accept what was happening and was obedient to God's will.

Mary's womb – God's temple

Here we should turn to Victoria Gillick who was given the following advice by the presiding judge: 'Any decision on the part of a girl to practise sex and contraception requires not only knowledge of the facts of life and of the dangers of pregnancy and disease, but also an understanding of the emotional and other consequences to her family, her male partner and herself. I doubt whether a girl under the age of 16 is capable of a balanced judgement to embark on frequent, regular or casual sexual intercourse fortified by the illusion that medical science can protect in mind and body and ignoring the danger of leaping from childhood to adulthood without the difficult formative transitional experiences of adolescence.'

Mary, the mother of Jesus Christ, was about the same age as Victoria Gillick's daughter when she conceived her Son, yet she had the maturity, judgement, and faith in those leading her to bend her will in obedience to God. Mary surely embodies what lies within all people, the potential to be centred on Christ and do His will.

Today, Man's attempts to control the functions of the womb through science are making many people uncomfortable, but they are wary of voicing their concerns because they know that society's moral framework is weak. Instead, they view with dismay the strong educational movement which supports doctors who usurp the parental role, and the devaluing of parental rights in relation to the sexual ethics of their own children. So confusion reigns, and moral values are at stake as society refuses to incorporate Christian principles into medical law and ethics. At the same time, phrases such as 'informed consent', and 'doctor/patient relationships' are commonplace. Society is turning every way in an attempt to establish a whole set of rules within a moral framework which denies Christ's teaching about the holiness of the womb.

Unfortunately, if we fail to recognise the womb as a holy place, we will not understand Christianity's message that Mary the Mother of the Word of God, represents an archetypal symbol of motherhood as protection for the whole world. St Paul expresses this belief in his letter to the turbulent Christian community in Corinth: 'Do you not realise that you are a temple of God with the Spirit of God living in you? If anybody should destroy the temple of God, God will destroy that person, because God's temple is holy; and you are that temple.' (1 Corinthians 3: 16,17)

When Mary conceived the Infant Jesus in her womb, she became the focal point of humanity and the Church which was to be. Jesus entered her womb and made that place holy by His presence. In the apse behind the altars of many Greek Byzantine churches, Mary is depicted with her arms outstretched in the protective attitude of a loving mother. This symbolises to the congregation the protection of Mary's womb, God's temple.

The holiness conferred on Mary's womb should be reflected in all those who seek the Christian way. Unfortunately, the purity of the example offered by the Virgin Mary is such that people tend to put it to one side as unique and therefore beyond emulation.

141

Moreover, today's society has become accustomed to pill-popping, fertility stimulants, hormone replacement therapy and any scientific treatment which will help a woman to conceive at will. The ideas of abortion, contraceptive aids and so on are now widely accepted, and many people feel that with a greater life expectancy, Man has finally achieved control over his body. Yet the list of potential ailments which may afflict women who use contraceptive aids makes depressing reading. Perhaps only by looking back at historical events will people be able to find a way forward in confidence and renewed faith.

St Irenaeus, Bishop of Lyons (130-200 AD) developed the doctrine of recapitulation which was a more full interpretation of Ephesians: 'For him [God] to act upon when the times had run their course: that he would bring everything together under Christ as head, everything in the heavens and everything on earth.' (Ephesians 1,10) Irenaeus saw the role of Jesus and Mary in union with God as one of recapitulation and an undoing of the work of Adam and Eve. In other words, God became Man in order that men might achieve divine status. St Paul explained this to the Ephesians: 'Now that is hardly the way you have learnt Christ, unless you failed to hear him properly when you were taught what the truth is in Jesus. You were to put aside your old self, which belongs to your old way or life and is corrupted by following illusory desires.' (Ephesians 4: 20-22)

Is there salvation through the Incarnation?

In the Incarnation, the eternal Son of God took human flesh from his human mother, and so was fully God and fully Man. Godhead and Manhood were united in His body without impairing the integrity or permanence of either.

Great controversy arose in the fourth and fifth centuries as Christians struggled to understand the Incarnation. Finally, the Definition of Chalcedon in Asia Minor resolved the arguments, and this has been accepted by Christian theologians of all schools to modern times. In the twentieth century, however, theologians began to apply philosophy to the study of the Incarnation.

142

Immanuel Kent (1724-1804), a German philosopher, promulgated the belief that all knowledge required an ingredient derived from the natural world. This is at the root of traditional metaphysics which claims to provide knowledge of subjects which wholly transcend nature. In other words, the three traditional proofs of God's existence (Ontological, Cosmological and Teleological) were declared invalid and were replaced by three central ideas: God, Freedom, Immortality, and these were interpreted as illusions. This led to the principle of immanence and to liberal theology, with an emphasis on the significance of culture and civilisation in the purpose of God and a desire to see the Incarnation in terms of mortality.

This outlook was further developed by Karl Barth (1886-1968), a Swiss Protestant theologian, who tried to lead theology back to a Reformational outlook. He was sure that the prophetic Biblical role recognised by the Reformers would affirm the supremacy and transcendent nature of God and the worthlessness of human reason. He also held that God's sole revelation was in Jesus Christ and in the Bible and these are God's only means of communicating with man. Such an outlook does away with any positive approach to science, culture, art and particularly to mysticism or emotions. The Incarnation has much less importance in this scenario.

This is when we turn to Mary, and her desire to serve God to such an extent that she achieved such holiness that she was worthy of any task God might choose to give her. Mary freely put herself at God's service so that the ultimate supremacy of love could become incarnate and living within her. Yet it is well-known that if a self-giving love is nurtured, it allows freedom of the spirit which permits an outpouring of love to all people. Mary was no exception. She reached a peak of holiness, for God filled her with His spirit of love to produce the Infant Christ. This was a phenomenon for all time and was meant to be normative for all humanity.

Unfortunately, many have challenged the supernatural character of faith, so when asked to believe that Christ truly came in human form through a virginal conception, humanity never ceases to speculate on how it could have happened. Many say it is beyond reason. Yet it is the ultimate gift of a loving God, and no dictum of Scripture can offer any grounds for evading the demands of the Incarnational imperative.

How did Mary achieve such a state of holiness if it was not hers at conception? Surely, it was conferred on her because of her extreme purity, which could not be defiled by Satan. Yet if Mary was truly to be the new Eve, and establish a new covenant with God, she first had to reveal the beauty of total goodness. Her battle was conducted at the source of creation – the womb.

Who is Satan? He is the serpent who seduced Eve and thus caused mankind's first sin, and he is therefore seen as the embodiment of evil. The challenge of evil is faced through divine wisdom which with the help of the Greek Fathers came to be a synonym for the Incarnate Word. St Paul offers an interesting insight into the nature of that wisdom: 'God's folly is wiser than human wisdom, and God's weakness is stronger than human strength. Consider, brothers, how you were called; not many of you were wise by human standards, not many influential, not many from noble families. No, God chose those who by human standards are fools to shame the wise; he chose those who by human standards are weak to shame the strong.' (1 Corinthians 1:25-27)

The devil was once described as 'the prince of emptiness'. This view must be reassuring to those who say there is no such thing as evil, but I see it another way: Satan sees himself as the prince of the unseen forces of darkness, only to be won by the wisdom of God when He became true God and true Man as Jesus Christ on earth. After all, in theological terminology, the devil is projected as the chief of the fallen angels, and the New Testament writers are clear about the spiritual assaults against Jesus Christ at the beginning of His public ministry.

Surely, Satan must by his nature attack the work of Creation, for the universe itself was created out of nothing by God. He must necessarily tempt Mary, for she was to bear Christ, and Christ would destroy Satan's work. Unfortunately, these days the traditional picture of creation is challenged by increased scientific knowledge and has caused extreme unease among orthodox Christians. Yet, for all the flamboyance which has

144

developed around the act of conception, scientists have hardly touched the fundamental philosophical questions which surround the notion of creation. These remain essentially unaffected. Nevertheless, Christians are uneasy about believing in the story of Genesis, because they cannot always relate to the vastness of the universe. Attempts to analyse the universe using modern physics often distress people, and it is unsettling to hear claims that the dimensions of the universe can be measured in both space and time.

Christ himself is beyond space and time, and yet in today's utilitarian outlook on life, people try to bring Christ within their own scientific outlook. Nowhere is this more apparent than in the field of creation. The impossibility of the task makes people feel helpless. And who is better placed to help than Mary who through her motherhood allowed the regeneration of God's children through a miraculous, virginal birth. St Augustine understood this: 'Is not the virginal womb of Mary the Mother of the Church?' Mary is the perfect example of regenerated humanity and the Church is her supreme offering to her son, created through receiving the Divinity of Christ in her womb through the Holy Spirit.

So what is the Christian Church? The early Christian Church claimed to be an organic whole which rested on the belief that it was inheritor of the promises made to Israel. This was implicit in Christ's teaching of a spiritual and invisible kingdom of God, the choosing of the Apostles and in the institution of sacramental rituals. In early times, the doctrine of the visible unity of the Church was accepted on all sides and a theology of the Church gradually developed which could identify the status of those in schism. Yet St Augustine (354-430) maintained that the sacraments were everywhere to be regarded as mystical acts of the Church which would maintain its structure.

However, since the schism between the eastern and western churches, which finally parted company in 1054, the two branches of Christendom each maintain that the other is in schism, while Anglicans and other Protestants do not accept the exclusive claim of any church. Only Mary, who brought humanity the gift of Jesus Christ and, through Him, the gift of the Holy Spirit at

Pentecost, can offer any solution, for in her role as the new Eve, she enabled the Redemption of humankind.

An illustration is offered in the way some churches celebrate Christmas with three Eucharists, of the night (normally midnight), of the dawn, and of the day, to symbolise the threefold birth of Christ: Christ eternally begotten of the Father, Christ born from the Virgin Mary's womb, and, mystically, Christ born in the souls of the faithful.

The ultimate choice to humankind

When people fail to achieve their objectives in life, they tend to deny the originals and try to present their acquaintance with a version of events which is grounded on an illusion but is presented in the best possible light. This is best seen in the phrase 'politically correct'. Yet, faced with the disintegration and diminution of the family, it is easy to feel insecure about the future of the younger generation.

The family is the object of unprecedented attacks, and there is almost a feeling of hostility to the concept of the father as wage-earner and guardian of his home. Why has society gone along with this anti-family and feminist approach without finding its own response?

Between 1971 and 1991 the number of lone-parent households in the UK more than doubled from 570,000 to 1,300,000, and the number of children living in such households has increased from 1 million to 2.2 million. It is common for young women to decide never to marry, and to believe that it is acceptable to have a child outside marriage. It is widely accepted that a child's needs are fully met by remaining with their mother if the marriage fails, irrespective of her conduct. Yet children need a stable environment in which to develop material, emotional and most of all spiritual security.

Regrettably, the entire population is being drawn into the politics of gender. A feminist interpretation of the law promotes the interests of women without reference to the needs of men, or men's rights to be protectors of their wives and children. Society

146

is being restructured to allow a mother and her children to constitute a legally supportable 'family'. Employment laws give women equal status to men, and little or no attention is paid to the domestic situation of women who have become mothers. More and more women are feeling stifled, as well as frightened, because of the demands placed on them by the law.

The Virgin Mary offers help. She has her place in God's plan of redemption. Nevertheless, attempts have been made to reduce her role to its absolute minimum and to avoid the spiritual maternity which Mary continues to exercise in the Church even today. Many people try to avoid Mary's maternal role in helping people to carry out their apostolate. Often, just at the times when people have needed clear guidance from theologians, they have instead fudged the issue. Instead, endless commissions try to organise people's thoughts into a conventional mould and nobody seems willing to speak out about the overwhelming example that the nations of the world have been set by Mary. This is the very nature of the birth of Christ, who came in human form in a planned pregnancy according to the will of God, and who acts as an example for all time and for all human conceptions.

The Catholic Church has presented its members with a vast abundance of doctrine about the place occupied by Mary in the mystery of Christ and his Church. Yet there is a reluctance to link her role with abortion. With every abortion committed, an unwanted child is killed. But did Mary and Joseph consider such an act when faced with the conception of Christ? No. They were prepared to be guided by the angelic host and listen to God's voice. In the same way, all people, even humanists, should be prepared to listen, if not to God, then to Christians. Christ came to be a bridge between God and humankind and this bridge is with us in every human conception, for every new life brings together both humankind and God.

Whether we like it or not, Mary was 'baptised in the Spirit' in order to lay the cornerstone of man's salvation which was Christ's conception. Here is the secret beginnings of the mystical body of Christ. The very fact that she was the mother of the Incarnate Word makes it possible for her and us to accept the words of Elizabeth: 'Of all women, you are the most blessed, and blessed is the fruit of your womb.' (Luke 1:42)

The message is loud and clear: are women prepared to permit God to bless the fruits of their wombs in the years to come?

REFERENCES

This book has been written deliberately with the minimum of references to make for easy reading. The main references though are:

The Jerusalem Bible
The Oxford Classical Dictionary
The Oxford Dictionary of the Christian Church
Sexual Chemistry, Dr. Ellen Grant
The Hutchinson Encyclopedia
The Family Medical Dictionary
Pregnancy, Gordon Bourne. FRCS. FRCOG.